Collection of

INSIDE STORIES

2010–2015

View Legal

MATTHEW BURGESS

National Library of Australia Cataloguing-in-Publication entry

Creator: Burgess, Matthew, author.

Title: Collection of inside stories 2010 - 2015 / Matthew Burgess; book designed by Dedicated Book Services.

ISBN: 9781925406085 (paperback)

ISBN: 9781925406092 (ebook : Kindle)

ISBN: 9781925406139 (ebook : epub)

Subjects: Burgess, Matthew.
View Legal (Firm)
Legal services—Australia.
Finance, Personal—Australia.
Assets (Accounting)—Australia.
Tax planning—Australia.
Estate planning—Australia.

Other Creators/Contributors: Dedicated Book Services, book designer.

Dewey Number: 347.00994

Published by D & M Fancy Pastry in 2015

Book Design by Dedicated Book Services

Table of Contents

Introduction

Matthew Burgess, Patrick Ellwood and Tara Lucke are co founders, with Naomi Arnold, of View Legal.

View Legal is results focused and passionate about delivering new solutions in a way that aligns with their 'SPS' – service and price satisfaction– guarantee leveraging from their founding of Australia's first virtual law firm.

As author of technical legal books, Matthew is widely recognised as constantly creating innovative strategies for the growth, management and protection of wealth.

Published legal books include:

1. The Nine Steps to a Complete Estate Plan.
2. The Seven Foundations of Business Succession.
3. Nine Essential Blue Journal Articles.
4. The Seven Key aspects of Testamentary Trusts.
5. The Seven Key aspects of SMSFs.
6. The Six Foundations of the Taxation of Trusts.

Chapter 1(a)

ASSET PROTECTION – PERSONAL

In times of peace – prepare for war

Posted 15 March 2010

Two weeks ago, I explained the importance of reviewing all loan accounts and unpaid present entitlements in the context of asset protection issues.

As flagged, that particular client situation was also problematic for a further two reasons. Those reasons were:

(1) Both the husband and wife were directors of the trading company, even though the wife had no active involvement in the business.
(2) Both the husband and wife were shareholders in the trading company.

Aside from the fact that the trading company had a large asset on its balance sheet (being the loan or UPE), the wife was also personally liable (automatically) due to her directorship. This issue could have been avoided by simply resigning her as a director. There is a further related practical tip in this regard that all advisers should be aware of and I will explore this further next week.

The second issue was that the husband (who had to be a director because of the level of involvement he had in the day-to-day operations of the business) personally owned shares in the trading company.

As a director, the husband carried personal liability and this means that his personal assets (including his shares in the trading company) were exposed.

Unlike the loan account issue, the strategies available in relation to the share ownership were ones that could only really be implemented subject to the bankruptcy clawback rules which (at a minimum) would delay any protection in relation to the shares until four years after divestment.

House transfers and real love

Posted 10 August 2010

Last week, I was reminded about the importance of proper planning when implementing asset protection strategies.

The particular scenario involved the potential clawback under the bankruptcy rules of a family home that had been gifted by a husband to a wife approximately 3½ years before a bankruptcy event. Many of you will be aware that changes to the bankruptcy rules extended the clawback period from 2 to 4 years a few years ago.

Whether the transfer could in fact be clawed back for this client was an issue which is as yet unresolved. The issue last week, however, was in relation to whether the value of the house as to today's date could be clawed back or whether its value 3½ years ago was the relevant value.

The question was quite critical because notwithstanding the intervening GFC, the value of the house had gone up by more than 20% over the 3½ year period.

As the original transfer had been crafted simply as a gift for 'natural love and affection', we had to advise the client that the house itself was the asset that would be exposed and therefore the value at today's date was at risk.

Next week, I will try to provide an example of how the original arrangement could have been structured differently to potentially limit the total value exposed under the clawback provisions.

The price of love

Posted 23 August 2010

Last week, we touched on a situation where the gifting of a family home was potentially exposed under the bankruptcy clawback rules.

As I mentioned last week, if the original transaction had been structured slightly differently, around 20% of the value of the property could have been protected.

In simple terms, instead of a straight gift of the property, the following steps could have been taken:

(1) The house could have been sold by the husband to his spouse for its market value 3½ years ago.
(2) The transaction should have been structured under a vendor finance arrangement.
(3) Following completion of the sale transaction, the husband could have forgiven the outstanding debt for 'natural love and affection'.
(4) Assuming that all steps would have been properly legally documented, then the wife would have had at least a reasonably arguable case that the capital growth in the asset since the date of the initial transfer would have been quarantined to her benefit and not available to creditors on the bankruptcy of her husband.

What difference does 1% make?

Posted 15 November 2010

Last week we were walking through an asset protection exercise with a business owner and one of the recommendations was that the family home (currently owned by the wife and husband as joint tenants) should be converted to tenants in common ownership 49% of the total interest of the house owned by the husband was then to be transferred to the wife.

An earlier post touches on the difference between owning an asset as joint tenants as opposed to tenants in common – a summary of the distinction is available via the 'learn' and then 'resources' tabs of the View Legal website (www.viewlegal.com.au).

Today's post focuses on the reasons why an at-risk spouse might retain a 1% interest in a property.

The main reasons that an at-risk spouse would retain a nominal percentage interest can include:

(1) Protection against spouse or relationship difficulties.
(2) Protection against the majority owner seeking to encumber the property. In particular, if there is (for example) a gambling issue that arises, no mortgage may be taken out over the property without the consent of the spouse who owns the nominal interest.
(3) For ease of security arrangements – often a financier will prefer to see the at-risk spouse's name on title documentation, even if their actual ownership interest is nominal.
(4) Stamp duty savings. This issue is not as relevant as in days gone by because generally there is no longer any substantial stamp duty benefit, even if both spouses retain an interest in the property.

In relation to stamp duty, it should be noted that in most states there are concessional provisions which apply where one spouse who owns 100% of a family home and transfers 50% (but no more or less) to their spouse and this is another concept that we may deal with in a future post.

Anti-avoidance rules to be amended from 1 March 2012

Posted 6 March 2012

Towards the end of last week the Federal Government announced that changes would be made to the general anti-avoidance tax provisions under part IVA.

The announcement was made in the context of the government's view that the provisions needed to 'be effective in counteracting tax avoidance schemes that are carried out as part of broader commercial transactions'.

In particular the proposed amendments are said to be designed to 'confirm that part IVA always intended to apply to commercial arrangements which have been implemented in a particular way to avoid tax. This also includes steps within broader commercial arrangements'.

The changes are said to be required because 'in recent cases, some taxpayers have argued successfully that they did not get a 'tax benefit' because, without the scheme, they would not have entered into an arrangement that attracted tax.

For example, they could have entered into another scheme that also avoided tax, deferred their arrangements indefinitely or done nothing at all.

Such an outcome can potentially undermine the overall effectiveness of Part IVA and so the Government will act to ensure such arguments will no longer be successful.'

The government has said that to ensure that the changes do not interfere with what are otherwise genuine commercial activities it will consult extensively as to how to best implement the new rules.

Specialist advice is also likely to be sought before preparing the first draft of the new legislation and throughout the redrafting process.

If you would like a full copy of the media release please email me.

When do 'gift and loan' arrangements need to be refreshed?

Posted 12 June 2012

As set out in earlier posts, and with thanks to the Television Education Network, today's post addresses the issue of 'When do 'gift and loan' arrangements need to be refreshed?' If you would like a copy of the video link please email me.

As usual, a transcript of the presentation for those that cannot (or choose not) to view the presentation is below –

There's two real reasons that the top up arrangement can come into effect.

The first one, and hopefully for most people, even in a post GFC environment, is that the actual underlying asset has gone up in value.

So in other words, you end up with a gap between the amount that was originally forwarded and the underlying asset value. So in that instance, there is obviously a desire to 'catch up' that gap or to remove that gap and that can be done by effectively recycling or regenerating a debt back to the trust and then making sure that the mortgage arrangements are updated to catch that additional amount.

The other reason that it might take place, and this particularly can arise in relation to master trusts, is where there's a feeling amongst the family unit that all arrangements are to be on a commercial basis.

In that instance, it's quite often the case that there are interest and principal repayments. So in that scenario, you'll start to get a gap between the level of security that the trust might have over the particular asset and the debt that's actually outstanding.

The critical point in relation to either of those scenarios, so in other words the asset going up in value or the debt being reduced, or for that matter, both things happening at once, is that whenever that gap is removed, you will generally find that there is wealth being moved away from an at-risk individual into a protected environment being the trust. Obviously in that scenario, in each and every instance that it takes place, you've potentially got to be aware of and advise the client, in relation to the application of the bankruptcy clawback provisions.

Adviser liability as a facilitator

Posted 22 October 2013

A recent post profiled a court decision where a lawyer was held liable for failing to have a client's estate planning instructions implemented within the space of a few days.

A number of advisers have made contact since the earlier post, concerned about their potential liability in similar circumstances.

While there does not appear to be any particular case exactly on point, we believe the broad position is as follows:

(1) advisers will potentially be liable for a failure to deliver to the standards that they promise, or alternatively, the standards expected of a competent adviser working in the area;

(2) it is therefore important that advisers ensure that both their promotional material and their retainers clearly articulate the level of service being provided and then ensure that they perform at least to that standard;

(3) in this regard, articulating what will not be done is often at least as important as setting out what will be done;
(4) it should generally be relatively easy for most advisers to discharge their professional obligation in the estate planning space by simply ensuring that the law firm that they partner with is engaged early in the process, and that the relevant law firm accepts the client's instructions;
(5) certainly, a large part of the success of our wholesale platform via View Legal seems to have come from the fact that its entire foundation is built on a collaborative approach with the adviser facilitating the process and the deliberate accepting of all legal risks associated with the process – this is in direct contrast to virtually all other alternatives that advisers have, such as online will providers and 'will kits';
(6) despite the above, there is an increasing amount of publicity about law firms marketing to disgruntled beneficiaries about their ability to sue advisers such as financial planners, accountants and risk advisers (in addition to suing other law firms), and in the vast majority of the promotional material, these law firms advertise their services on a 'no win no fee' basis – this trend would seem to suggest there will be increasing litigation in the area; and
(7) in this context, the recent situation where the solicitor was sued for negligence is a timely reminder for all advisers to have a bias towards compliance, best practice and continual improvement of their service offering.

PPSA transitional arrangements end on 30 January 2014

Posted 8 October 2013

A post from February 2012 considered the Personal Property Securities Act 2009 (Cth) (PPSA) which commenced some 18 months ago.

Today's post focuses on one of the upcoming critical aspects of the regime.

The PPSA is the national system for personal property securities in Australia and replaced many state, territory and Commonwealth registers of personal property securities.

Central to this system is the Personal Property Securities Register (PPSR) where details of security interests in personal property can be registered and searched.

To give creditors an opportunity to adjust to the new regime, the PPSA included transitional provisions. The principal object of these provisions was to maintain priority between security interests that existed before the PPSA commenced on 30 January 2012 for two years. These interests are known as 'transitional security interests'.

This two year transitional period ends on 30 January 2014.

To ensure transitional security interests continue to be protected they should be reviewed to ensure they are validly registered on the PPSR by 30 January 2014. There is no PPSR fee to register a transitional security interest.

One remedy where trust distributions prove problematic

Posted 15 October 2013

For those that do not otherwise have access to the Weekly Tax Bulletin, the article from last week is extracted below.

A recent article in this Bulletin focused on the critical need to "read the deed" whenever making trust distributions (see 2013 WTB 38 [1642]).

Even where distributions are made validly to a potential beneficiary, they can prove extremely problematic from an asset protection perspective.

One scenario that seems to arise regularly in this regard is the distribution by a trust to a corporate beneficiary, the shares in which are owned personally by an at-risk individual.

Often, the difficulties with this ownership structure are not identified until after many years of distributions have been made to the bucket company, and anecdotally, the issue is often first identified at a point which is too late, for example, just before litigation proceedings are to commence against the relevant shareholder.

Where this ownership structure is identified and assessed to be inappropriate, the first critical step is to ensure that any future distributions to a corporate beneficiary are directed to a newly established company, the shares in which are owned by a non-risk entity (e.g. a passive family trust).

However, resolving the historical distributions is generally not as simple.

Depending on the circumstances, some form of dividend access share or discretionary dividend share may provide a pathway to remedy the historic distributions, although it will be important to consider the ATO's recent guidance in Draft Taxation Determination TD 2013/D5 (see 2013 WTB 24 [1092]) and Taxpayer Alert TA 2012/4 (see 2012 WTB 30 [1194]) which warned taxpayers of arrangements where accumulated profits of a private company are distributed substantially tax-free to an entity associated with the ordinary shareholders of the private company.

Similarly, since the introduction of the Personal Property Securities Act 2009 (PPSA), steps can often be taken to grant a security interest over the at-risk shares to a low risk related entity.

Broadly, this solution can be achieved by a "gift and loan back" style arrangement, whereby:

(1) the at-risk individual gifts a cash amount equal to the gross value of the shares to a protected environment (e.g. a passive family trust);
(2) the family trust subsequently lends the gifted amount back to the at-risk individual; and
(3) the family trust simultaneously registers a security interest over the shares on the PPS register to secure repayment of the loan. Subject to certain conditions (such as the family trust establishing "control" over the shares) the family trust's interest in the shares should be protected under the PPSA.

The advantages of utilising a gift and loan back, compared to a straight transfer of the shares in the corporate beneficiary can include:

(1) the arrangement achieves broadly equivalent protection for the asset compared with a straight transfer; and
(2) as there is no change in the legal ownership of the shares, transfer duty (where applicable) and capital gains tax will generally not apply. The only transaction cost should be the PPSR registration fee.

The disadvantages of utilising a gift and loan back approach, compared to a straight transfer of the shares can include:

(1) the arrangement is more complex than a simple transfer, and involves the preparation of additional documentation (including a deed of gift, loan agreement and security documentation);
(2) it only protects the amount of net equity in the asset at the time of the gifting, however as mentioned above, there should not be any further distributions made to the inappropriately structured corporate beneficiary; and
(3) the arrangement is subject to the bankruptcy clawback rules and specialist advice should be obtained in relation to the operation of these provisions.

Family courts' power to adjust inheritance rights

Posted 29 January 2013

With thanks to co View Legal director Tara Lucke, this week's post looks at the widely publicised High Court judgment of Stanford v Stanford (2012) HCA 52 from the end of 2012 and the Family Courts' powers to potentially displace the distribution of assets under an estate plan. A link to the full copy of the decision is as follows:

http://www.austlii.edu.au/au/cases/cth/HCA/2012/52.html

As many will be aware the brief facts were that Mr and Mrs Stanford had no children together, although both had children from previous relationships. The Stanford's had both crafted their estate plans to provide for their respective children, without making provision for each other, other than a life tenancy in the family home. The house was owned solely in the name of Mr Stanford (he had bought it before the marriage), although it had been lived in by the couple for over 40 years.

Critically, Mrs Stanford appointed her children, not Mr Stanford, under her guardian and attorney documents.

Due to ill health and mental incapacity, Mrs Stanford was moved into residential care. Despite no suggestion that the couple were anything other than happily married, on her mother's incapacity Mrs Stanford's daughter initiated proceedings in the Family Court (as Mrs Stanford's legal guardian) seeking orders for equal division of the marital property (the main asset was the family home) between Mr and Mrs Stanford.

The initial Judge ordered that Mr Stanford pay a fixed sum of approximately half the value of the marital property to Mrs Stanford, which payment would have effectively passed directly to her guardians. To fund the payment the family home would have needed to be sold, forcing Mr Stanford to leave the house.

Mr Stanford appealed the decision, however Mrs Stanford passed away before judgment was delivered by the Court of Appeal. The Court of Appeal ultimately decided that Mrs Stanford's legal personal representatives should receive the fixed sum upon the death of Mr Stanford. This decision effectively altered the distribution of Mr Stanford's estate (which Mrs Stanford had agreed with while she had capacity) under his will as the house (following his wife's death) would have otherwise passed to his children.

The decision of the Court of Appeal was ultimately set aside on appeal to the High Court, on the basis that the order was not just and equitable. However, importantly, the High Court confirmed that the death of a party to a marriage 'does not transform the nature of the claim (for example, into a claim by the beneficiaries of the wife's estate)'.

In other words, the right of a guardian or attorney to commence property settlement proceedings was effectively confirmed, even where (as here) they would have no entitlement to challenge the estate of their step father.

The decision highlights the risks that in some cases, particularly in relation to blended families, estate distributions may be fundamentally altered by way of 'preemptive' proceedings through the family law court.

Leading Gift and Loan Back Case

Posted 27 March 2014

Other posts have dealt with various aspects of gift and loan back arrangements (see ***http://blog.viewlegal.com.au/2012/05/family-court-case-on-distinction.html*** and ***http://blog.viewlegal.com.au/2013/10/one-remedy-where-trust-distributions.html***).

Arguably, the leading case in relation to gift and loan back arrangements is Atia v Nusbaum [2011] QSC044. As usual, a link to the full decision is as follows –

http://www.austlii.edu.au/cgi-bin/sinodisp/au/cases/qld/QSC/2011/44.html.

In summary the circumstances of this case were as follows:

(1) Dr Atia (a cosmetic surgeon) entered into a gift and loan back style arrangement with his mother;
(2) when Dr Atia's mother subsequently called in the debt, Dr Atia argued that the loan and mortgage were not intended to be actually binding and were only a pretence to protect against situations where Dr Atia was sued professionally;
(3) in particular, Dr Atia argued that his mother was only calling in the debt secured by the mortgage because he had married his girlfriend against his mother's express wishes;
(4) the court found that all aspects of the legal documentation, including a deed of gift, loan agreement and registered mortgage, had been validly signed; and
(5) the court confirmed that the legal effect of the documentation signed was exactly as the parties intended it to be and there was no mistake or sham involved. This meant that Dr Atia's mother was allowed to enforce recoverability of the debt, and if necessary, exercise her rights under the registered mortgage.

How gift and loan back arrangements work?

Posted 1 April 2014

Previous posts have touched on various aspects of the gift and loan back strategy (see ***http://blog.viewlegal.com.au/2012/05/family-court-case-on-distinction.html*** and ***http://blog.viewlegal.com.au/2013/10/one-remedy-where-trust-distributions.html***).

Recently, and as touched on last week regarding Atia's case, one of the key aspects of the enforceability of this style of arrangement is that all documentation is drafted correctly and duly signed and processed.

In this regard, the main critical steps that need to be followed are set out below with an example.

The 'gift and loan back' approach involves the owner of an asset gifting an amount equal to their equity in the property or shares in a company to a family trust (or low risk spouse).

The family trust then lends an amount of money to the owner and takes a secured mortgage over the property or registers a security interest on the Personal Property Securities Register over the shares.

Example

Using property as an example, assume that Anne holds 100% of an investment property and the current value of the home is $1,500,000. There is an existing mortgage of $500,000 owing to her financier.

Step 1: Anne gifts the amount of her equity in the property to a trust

Step 2: The trust subsequently lends the amount back to Anne and takes security over property

Subdivision EA & Gift/Loan Back Arrangements

Posted 8 April 2014

Recent posts have touched on various aspects of the 'gift and loan back' arrangement.

Recently we had a situation where historically a gift and loan back arrangement had been entered into, however the provisions of the Tax Act under subdivision EA had been ignored.

While there has been some significant dilution of the circumstances where subdivision EA will apply given the Tax Office's approach to unpaid present entitlements, in the situation we were looking at it remained potentially relevant.

In particular, the second 'tranche' of the gift and loan back arrangement involving a loan out of a trust was problematic because at the time the loan was made, there was an unpaid distribution to a corporate beneficiary.

We are working with the relevant adviser to determine the most appropriate approach moving forward, however the example was a timely reminder that in any structuring exercise, it is critical to consider all potential transaction costs and in particular those that are not immediately obvious.

Gift and Loan Back Arrangements – Some Frequently Asked Questions

Posted 15 April 2014

Recent posts have looked at various aspects of the 'gift and loan back' strategy (***http://blog.viewlegal.com.au/2014/03/leading-gift-and-loan-back-case.html*** and ***http://blog.viewlegal.com.au/2014/04/subdivision-ea-giftloan-back.html***)

While there are a myriad of potential issues that always need to be considered, some of the key aspects include:

(1) care should always be taken to ensure that the trust which will make the secured loan does not itself conduct risky activities (for example, run a business).

(2) while the arrangement can be entered into without registering a mortgage, if this step is not taken, the trust that has made the loan will simply be an unsecured creditor.

(3) the impact of the arrangement in relation to potentially accessing the small business tax concessions should always be carefully considered, because while a family home will generally be excluded from the $6 million test, a secured loan will generally be included if the trust is an affiliate or 'connected entity' under the Tax Act (which will typically be the case).

(4) to the extent that a third party financier already has a mortgage over the property, they will generally require a deed of priority securing their lendings (to whatever level they may be from time to time) as a first priority before the trust's second mortgage.

(5) As flagged in previous posts (***http://blog.viewlegal.com.au/2013/10/one-remedy-where-trust-distributions.html***) if no real property is available for registering security over, personal property can be used via the Personal Property Security Register.

Bankruptcy Clawback – A Leading Case

Posted 22 April 2014

In any asset protection exercise, the impact of the 'clawback' rules under the bankruptcy legislation needs to be carefully considered.

One key aspect in this regard is whether a decision by a person to divest themselves of assets was done for the main purpose of defeating creditors.

Recently, I was reminded of arguably the leading case in this area, which is now over 80 years old, namely Williams v Lloyd [1934] HCA1. As usual, a link to the full copy of the decision is as follows – ***http://www.austlii.edu.au/cgi-bin/sinodisp/au/cases/cth/HCA/1934/1.html?stem=0&synonyms=0&query=title***

In this case, a bankrupt transferred assets to family members while he was solvent, but knowing that he was likely to start engaging in a 'risky' business activity in the future.

The court held that the transfers could not be clawed back and the key aspect of the decision was as follows –

'Once it is acknowledged, as upon the evidence I think it must be, that in 1926 the bankrupt was in a perfectly sound financial position and had nothing to fear, subsequent conduct and events form an insufficient basis for a finding that the documents were shams, or that he had an intent to defraud his creditors, or that they were made subject to a suspensory condition allowing them to take effect only in case of attack by creditors.'

What strategies are there available to protect at risk beneficiaries?

Posted 27 June 2014

As set out in earlier posts, and with thanks to the Television Education Network, today's post addresses the issue of 'What strategies are there available to protect at risk beneficiaries?' at the following link – ***http://youtu.be/Joz2vYxhcDY***

As usual, a transcript of the presentation for those that cannot (or choose not) to view the presentation is below –

The obvious solution is to try to minimise the number of distributions that go to the at risk beneficiary. That's obviously a lot easier said than done. Particularly from a tax perspective, there is a bias towards making sure that the income does flow out to an individual beneficiary, particularly if there's a capital gain to be distributed.

Leaving that to one side, there are other ways to manage it, the biggest one seen in practice is making sure that the recipient beneficiary is themselves not exposed.

The classic example would be using a corporate beneficiary or company as the recipient. In that scenario, it's important to remember that the ownership structure of the shares in that company is going to be vital.

You don't want to create a situation where even though the beneficiary exposed doesn't directly have the asset or the income distributed to them, they're the shareholder of the company, which is the recipient beneficiary. The risk is that the wealth is effectively in just as exposed a position as it would have otherwise been.

Chapter 1(b)

ASSET PROTECTION – FAMILY LAW

Do prenups actually work?

Posted 14 March 2011

The above question was posed to me during the week and, unfortunately, when I was told to make my answer succinct, the only thing that easily came to mind was 'it depends'.

Many advisers will be aware that prenups (or as they are more technically termed in Australia 'binding financial agreements') have been available for around 10 years now.

There have been a number of changes to the way in which the rules in this area work and the most significant of these changes occurred towards the end of last year.

While there were a number of quite heavily publicised cases where what otherwise appeared to be binding agreements were held to be invalid, the changes made towards the end of last year have generally been seen to be positive steps to ensure that disgruntled spouses cannot extract themselves from previously made promises on the basis of a legal technicality.

Prenups and the need for independent advice

Posted 1 August 2011

An interesting issue came up recently in relation to a 'prenuptial agreement (more technically referred to as a 'binding financial agreement')'.

In particular, as many would know, the need for both parties to the relationship to obtain independent legal advice was brought into question because often one party chose not to follow the advice that was provided.

Based on recent cases, it seems clear that:

(1) There is no need for independent advice to be accepted or followed for the requirement that independent advice is sought, to be satisfied.

(2) It could therefore be a situation where the advice provided by the independent lawyer is incorrect and even in these circumstances, the criteria that independent advice be sought, may still be satisfied.

What is a spouse?

Posted 15 August 2011

The issue that what kind of relationship satisfies the definition of a 'spouse' comes up very regularly.

The Tax Act sets out one of the most used definitions in this regard and I thought it useful this week to extract that definition in its entirety, given that it has been amended relatively recently.

A "*spouse*" of an individual includes:

a another individual (whether of the same sex or a different sex) with whom the individual is in a relationship that is registered under a State law or Territory law prescribed for the purposes of section 22B of the *Acts Interpretation Act 1901* as a kind of relationship prescribed for the purposes of that section; and
b another individual who, although not legally married to the individual, lives with the individual on a genuine domestic basis in a relationship as a couple.

The link to the above definition is as follows:

http://www.austlii.edu.au/au/legis/cth/consol_act/itaa1997240/s995.1.html

What is a de facto?

Posted 22 August 2011

Following on from last week's post, I thought it would be useful to also summarise the definition of 'de facto'.

This particular definition is taken from the Family Law Act (Section 4AA).

In summary, a person will be in a de facto relationship with another person, if:

a the persons are not legally married to each other; and
b the persons are not related by family (see subsection (6)); and
c having regard to all the circumstances of their relationship, they have a relationship as a couple living together on a genuine domestic basis.

A link to the above definition is as follows:

http://www.austlii.edu.au/au/legis/cth/consol_act/fla1975114/s4aa.html

De facto relationships – further examples

Posted 29 August 2011

Further to last week's post, the list below sets out some of the specific circumstances that are taken into account by the courts to determine whether a relationship does amount to a de facto relationship.

Circumstances of the relationship taken into consideration include any or all of the following:

a the duration of the relationship;
b the nature and extent of their common residence;
c whether a sexual relationship exists;
d the degree of financial dependence or interdependence, and any arrangements for financial support, between them;
e the ownership, use and acquisition of their property;
f the degree of mutual commitment to a shared life;
g whether the relationship is or was registered under a prescribed law of a State or Territory as a prescribed kind of relationship;
h the care and support of children; and
i the reputation and public aspects of the relationship.

A link to the above definition is as follows:

http://www.austlii.edu.au/au/legis/cth/consol_act/fla1975114/s4aa.html

Being a 'kept woman' may not be a de facto relationship

Posted 5 September 2011

Following last week's post, I was reminded of a case from earlier this year that involved a lady who had been a part of a secret intimate relationship with a married family man for 17 years.

According to her evidence, she and the man involved 'spent time together at various times in various places, had a sexual relationship, and expressed love and affection for each other'. The argument being that this was a 'de facto relationship' within the meaning of s4AA of the Family Law Act.

The man denied 'any such relationship', and instead claimed it was simply 'an affair' and the lady was a 'kept woman'. Both parties agreed that they travelled overseas together and the man paid the lady $24,000 to help her buy a home and $2,000 monthly, increasing progressively to $3,000 a month.

While the court rejected the man's argument that 'exclusivity' was necessary for a de facto relationship to exist, the facts here did not support the lady's argument that they were de factos.

The quote that best captured the decision here was as follows:

> "the key to that definition (i.e. de facto) is the manifestation of a relationship where both the parties have so merged their lives that they were, for all practical purposes 'living together' as a couple on a genuine domestic basis. It is the manifestation of 'coupledom' which involves the merger of two lives as just described, that is the core of a de facto relationship as defined and to which each of the statutory factors (and others that want to apply to a particular relationship) are directed".

What is an 'interdependency relationship'?

Posted 12 September 2011

Following on from last week's post, one issue that was raised with me related to the concept of an 'interdependency relationship' under the superannuation rules.

Again, for those who have not had cause to look at it recently, this definition is worth reviewing closely and an extract of it is included below.

Two persons (whether or not related by family) have an interdependency relationship under this section if:

a they have a close personal relationship; and
b they live together; and
c one or each of them provides the other with financial support; and
d one or each of them provides the other with domestic support and personal care.

In addition, 2 persons (whether or not related by family) also have an interdependency relationship under this section if:

a they have a close personal relationship; and
b they do not satisfy one or more of the requirements of an interdependency relationship mentioned in paragraphs (1)(b), (c) and (d); and

c the reason they do not satisfy those requirements is that either or both of them suffer from a physical, intellectual or psychiatric disability.

A link the above definition is as follows:

http://www.austlii.edu.au/au/legis/cth/consol_act/itaa1997240/s302.200.html

Interdependency relationship – further examples

Posted 19 September 2011

Following on from last week's post, some comments were received in relation to the lack of cases in this relatively new area of law.

Interestingly, the superannuation legislation (for those particularly interested, the actual regulation is 1.04AAAA) sets out a number of tests in relation to whether a relationship between two people amounts to an interdependency relationship.

In summary, the tests include:

a the duration of the relationship;
b whether or not a sexual relationship exists;
c the ownership, use and acquisition of property;
d the degree of mutual commitment to a shared life;
e the care and support of children;
f the reputation and public aspects of the relationship;
g the degree of emotional support;
h the extent to which the relationship is one of mere convenience; and
i any evidence suggesting that the parties intend the relationship to be permanent.

A link the above definition is as follows:

http://www.austlii.edu.au/au/legis/cth/consol_reg/sir1994582/s1.04aaaa.html

As you will see, many of these themes are similar to the definition of what a de facto relationship is, which were summarised in a post a few weeks ago.

'Look through' powers of the Family Court

Posted 14 July 2015

As set out in earlier posts, and with thanks to the Television Education Network, today's post addresses the issue of 'Look through' powers of the Family Court' at the following link– ***https://www.youtube.com/watch?v=4I57VXYU0w4&feature=youtu.be***

As usual, a transcript of the presentation for those that cannot (or choose not) to view the presentation is below –

> The ultimate rationale in relation to the look through powers of the Family Court which are extraordinarily wide – the Family Court has powers that do not exist in other area of the law– is public policy.
>
> This is because it is seen as inequitable that a party who has been in a longstanding relationship has access to assets that they can effectively deal with as their own via a trust structure, but then suddenly those assets are completely ignored in a property settlement.
>
> The rules are driven by public policy and this is why the concept of 'continuum' as to the way the courts deal with trusts is so relevant. The answer to the question 'is that asset protected?' in many situations will ultimately often be 'it depends'. And it depends on the court's perception and interpretation as to how that overriding and overarching public policy framework applies to any particular factual scenario.

Sham trusts and the Family Court

Posted 28 July 2015

As set out in earlier posts, and with thanks to the ***Television Education Network***, today's post addresses the issue of 'Sham trusts' at the following link –

https://www.youtube.com/watch?v=ERpGAlIf_ro&feature=youtu.be

As usual, a transcript of the presentation for those that cannot (or choose not) to view the presentation is below –

> Sham Trusts are probably the most interesting aspect of what is otherwise a very interesting topic in terms of structuring of trusts from an asset protection perspective under the family law provisions.

Ultimately, a sham trust will be held to exist where there has been a deliberate and focused attempt by the people behind the trust to actually completely mislead and deceive anyone else that might have come into contact with it, whether it be other beneficiaries, former spouses or indeed the court.

Where a sham trust is held to exist, what the court is empowered to do is just completely ignore it as if the trust is a complete nullity. Obviously this is a very radical power given to courts, in that despite the legal documentation, the court can just completely ignore it.

What the cases have shown is that while the Family Court certainly has the power to deem a trust to be a sham, they are very reticent to do so, unless there is very clear evidence to support such a finding.

Binding financial agreements and trusts

Posted 17 November 2015

As set out in earlier posts, and with thanks to the Television Education Network, today's post addresses the issue of 'Binding financial agreements and trusts' at the following link–

https://www.youtube.com/watch?v=dS8CjyW0hUY

As usual, a transcript of the presentation for those that cannot (or choose not) to view the presentation is below –

There is no doubt that a properly crafted binding financial agreement or 'BFA' provides the best protection from an asset protection perspective available.

The difficulty is that even despite the changes that the government has brought in to make binding financial agreements more robust, the reality is there is a level of scepticism about just how useful BFAs are actually going to be, because there seem to be so many ways in which they can be unwound on a technicality.

While the general view is that they are the ideal outcome in terms of protecting wealth, the conservative view would always be that steps are taken to complement the BFA and to try and ensure the assets are ultimately quarantined on a relationship breakdown.

One obvious example is to implement testamentary discretionary trusts under the estate plan, regardless of whether a BFA is in existence.

Chapter 1(c)

ASSET PROTECTION – FAMILY LAW CASES

Spry – one year on

Posted 3 October 2011

Undoubtedly, the highest profile family law case (at least involving trusts from 2010) was the Spry case.

While the actual scenario was somewhat unique and obviously the decision became one of the highest profiled decisions issued by the High Court in this space in recent years, the actual implications of the case may not in fact be as far reaching as first thought.

In particular, what many advisers in this area are seeing is that a number of the aspects of the decision can be explained by the particularly aggressive and arguably misleading approach that the husband took in relation to attempting to remove assets from the pool that could be distributed to his former wife.

Unless something else comes up during the week, next post I will summarise a recent family law decision that further confirms that the Spry decision may not be as concerning as many commentators first thought.

Family law case excludes assets owned by a family trust

Posted 10 October 2011

As mentioned in last week's post, a family law case from earlier this year involving a family trust has received an amount of attention given the decision seems somewhat at odds with the High Court's decision in Spry.

The more recent case named *Keach & Keach and Ors* [2011] FamCA 192 – (if you would like a copy of the case please email me) focused on a family trust that the father of the divorcing husband had established.

The father admitted that among other things, his reason for setting up the trust was to keep the assets as far away from the reach of the family court as possible.

The divorcing wife argued that the assets of the trust should be available to her on a property settlement as her former husband effectively treated them as his own.

The court held that the assets should be ignored on the property settlement. Effectively, the only time that the legal documents and arrangements could be ignored was where they were a sham or a 'mere puppet'. In all other instances, the family court cannot ignore the interests of third parties in the property, nor the existence of conditions or covenants that limit the rights of the party who owns it.

Further comments on assets protected by a family trust on marriage breakdown

Posted 17 October 2011

Further to last week's post, some feedback was received about other aspects of the decision mentioned (Keach & Keach and Others).

To provide some more context to the main conclusion of the case mentioned last week, it is worth noting that:

(1) The relevant trust was established by the father of the divorcing husband.
(2) The father had all practical control over the trust as well as legal control.
(3) While the main asset of the trust (being a home that the husband and wife were living in) was allegedly used by the husband 'as if it were his own', this did not change the legal ownership position.
(4) In order for an arrangement to be a sham (and therefore, for example, for the trust's ownership to be ignored), it must be shown that all relevant parties had the common intention to mislead others.
(5) Even if the husband was conducting himself as if he were the owner, unless it could be shown that the husband's father intended the arrangement to be a sham, then there was no access to the assets of the trust.
(6) Here the evidence was in fact the opposite – i.e. the husband's father deliberately structured the arrangements to ensure that he retained control and direction of the trust. On this basis, the assets of the trust could not be considered as assets of the marriage.

Another family law case on trusts

Posted 12 March 2012

Posts made in October 2011 focused on a high profile family law case involving a family trust (Keach).

In that case, the assets of a family trust were essentially protected on a property settlement.

Towards the end of last year, the case Harris v Harris (if you would like a copy of the case please email me) provided further context to the general attitude of the Family Court in relation to traditional trust structures.

The outcomes of both cases can be contrasted with the outcomes in cases involving arrangements that the Court believes are unconscionably designed to hide assets (for example, the case of the Kennon v Spry, also featured in the posts during the latter half of 2011).

In brief terms, the Harris case involved a trust established by the husband's father.

At the relevant time, the appointor of the trust was the husband's mother and the controllers of the trustee company were the husband's mother, a son from a previous relationship and a friend.

The main asset of the trust was a business which it was accepted was run on a day-to-day basis by the husband and wife.

The main beneficiaries of the trust were the husband's parents and their children (i.e. the husband and his siblings).

Distributions from the trust had been amongst the entire family group (including the wife), although the distributions to the wife ceased on separation with the husband.

In summary, the Court held:

(1) The trust and its assets were not an asset of the marriage.
(2) At most, the trust should be considered a significant financial resource for the husband.
(3) If a party to the marriage is not directly the appointor or in control of the trustee, then they do not have direct control.
(4) In order for there to be indirect control by a beneficiary, there must effectively be a situation where someone who has direct control is the mere puppet of the beneficiary.
(5) In order to demonstrate indirect control (e.g. through a 'puppet' scenario), there must be clear evidence to support the argument and merely reviewing a history of trust distributions of itself will not be sufficient.

Contribution assessments in family law cases

Posted 26 March 2012

The posts for the last 2 weeks have focused on the decision from the end of 2011 of Harris.

One final aspect of the case that it is worth highlighting involved the comments made by the Court about the 'contribution' that the parties to the marriage, and their respective families, made to growing the asset base during the course of the relationship.

As many will be aware, once the court has determined the property that satisfies the definition of being an 'asset' of the marriage and then in turn the property that is a 'resource', there is a need to determine the contribution the parties have made to creating the wealth.

In the Harris case, the appeal court expressly directed that in the retrial (which is yet to take place) the judge must be careful to ensure that adequate weight is given to the husband and his parents in terms of building up the value of the business that was owned by the family trust at the centre of the dispute.

This direction was as a result of the initial trial judge's decision to simply ignore the contribution that had been made by the husband and his parents over many years, both before the marriage and during the course of it.

Family court case on the distinction between a loan and a gift

Posted 21 May 2012

We are increasingly seeing advisers and clients alike, focussing (very deliberately) on the way in which they advance monies to their children to assist with, for example, the purchase of a family home.

Today's post looks at a recent case, which was decided last year, and provides a useful example of the distinction between gifting and lending monies from a family law perspective, particularly in the event of a relationship breakdown.

The case of *Pelly & Nolan* [2011] involved a situation where the husband's father advanced approximately $520,000 to 'help his son out'. The initial advance was $320,000 to assist the son and his young family purchase a property. Additional advances were also made to assist with general living expenses totalling approximately $200,000.

The evidence in the case suggested that the father sought repayment for only the $320,000 advanced relating to the property acquisition and not the monies advanced for general living expenses.

As the initial advance was facilitated by a loan agreement and for the purpose of assisting with the property purchase, the court held that such advance was enforceable, even though no interest on the loan had been demanded nor paid.

In relation to the additional $200,000 advanced, there was no evidence to suggest that a repayment would be enforced by the father.

In the circumstances therefore, the court held that the $320,000 advance was indeed a loan and thus a liability that needed to be deducted from the matrimonial assets; whereas the $200,000 advance would be included as property for distribution to the wife (although the fact that it had been contributed by the husband's father would be taken into account).

Please email me if you would like a copy of this case.

Assets of a family trust not necessarily at risk on a matrimonial breakdown

Posted 17 September 2012

The post this week focuses on another recent decision of the Family Court concerning trusts.

The case is *Morton V Morton* [2012] FamCA 30. If you would like a copy of the case please email me.

Essentially, the case confirms that, where appropriately structured, the assets of a family trust will not be considered matrimonial property on a relationship breakdown.

The decision highlights the importance of carefully considering the most appropriate structure for trust arrangements to achieve the objectives of the parties, particularly in the context of a relationship breakdown.

As explored in more detail below, the particular decision here largely rejected arguments based on the Kennon v Spry decision, which, at the time, caused many advisers to believe that family trusts provided little (and perhaps no) protection on a relationship breakdown.

Facts of the case

The case involved a property settlement in the divorce between Mr and Mrs Morton (pseudonym), a couple from Sydney who had been married for approximately 10 years. There were no children of the marriage.

At the time of the divorce, the husband was a beneficiary of a discretionary trust, the Morton Trust (Trust).

The beneficiaries of the trust included the Husband (H) and his brother (HB), their mother, any grandchildren or remoter relatives and any companies or trusts in which H or HB had an interest.

The trustee company, J Pty Ltd (Trustee) had two ordinary shares, one owned by each of the brothers. The brothers were both the directors of the Trustee.

The brothers jointly were the appointors of the Trust.

The Trust had a 'bucket company', T Pty Ltd (Bucket Co), which was owned 100% by Trustee on behalf of the Trust. There were unpaid present entitlements (UPEs) owing to Bucket Co. HB was the sole director of Bucket Co.

The wife claimed that, between them, H and HB each effectively had a 50% share in the assets of the Trust and Bucket Co. As such, H's interest in the Trust and Bucket Co (half of its assets) should be treated as his property, and therefore added to his pool of assets for division under the property settlement.

Issues

The wife argued that H, as a director of Trustee, had 'control' of the Trust and in turn Bucket Co. However, H argued that, as HB was appointed and acted in the same capacity as a director, neither H nor HB had control of the Trustee, and their rights were equal (i.e. neither brother had effective control).

The fact that the brothers were joint appointors and had the power to remove and appoint a trustee was also considered.

The court held that there was a bona fide trust arrangement. While (as most families would hope) there was a 'warm and loving relationship' between the brothers and there had been inter-mixing of funds – not only their own personal funds, but funds from various entities from which the Trust received distributions – there was insufficient evidence to convince the judge that H had sufficient control over the Trust and Bucket Co to simply treat those assets as his.

It was held that the interest in the Trust and the UPEs in Bucket Co should be excluded from the husband's asset pool. The interest in the Trust was treated as a 'financial resource'. However, this was not a contentious issue, H had previously conceded that the interest in the Trust should be treated as such.

Implications of the decision

In considering the relevance of Kennon v Spry (2008) 238 CLR 366, the court was satisfied on the evidence that the Trust did not hold the assets as an 'alter ego' of H. As such, the judge found that the assets of the Trust were not to be treated as H's assets – ultimately he was merely a potential beneficiary and did not in fact control the Trust.

Had it not have been for the husband's brother, who was appointed as co-director of Trustee and co-appointor for the Trust, the outcome of this case may have been different.

The decision demonstrates that when establishing trusts and related entities, thought should be given to:

- relinquishing some control at a shareholder level
- appointing multiple directors of any trustee company, and
- appointing more than one appointor and requiring that they act jointly.

Deferral of property settlements

Posted 12 November 2012

This week's post looks at a recent Family Court case – *Pratt* [2012] FamCAFC 81 (13 June 2012). A link to the full copy of the decision is as follows:

http://www.austlii.edu.au/au/cases/cth/FamCAFC/2012/81.html

The husband and wife were graziers. The main issue in dispute was that a valuer had confirmed there had been a $10 million decrease in value of their two cattle stations over recent years as a result of exceptional circumstances (such as the restrictions on live cattle export). The parties agreed that as a result, the bank debt over the properties substantially exceeded the value of the land.

The wife sought a three year adjournment under the Family Law Act to enable a 'just and equitable property settlement', on the basis of the valuer's statement that the land should increase in value substantially over the next two years, as market conditions return to normal.

The husband opposed the delay on the basis that the parties' debts exceeded their assets and he could not meet the interest owed to the bank. The adjournment was originally granted but appealed by the husband.

Normally an adjournment is only available where a 'significant change' in financial circumstances is likely and the delay will probably do justice, more so than an immediate division of property.

Ultimately, the Court accepted the husband's argument and ordered that the property settlement be finalised immediately. A key aspect of the decision to deny an adjournment was the failure in the original decision to factor in the cost of maintaining an increasing debt through interest on the loan facility and the ongoing costs of running the properties.

In other words, it was held that in order to delay a property settlement, all relevant financial issues must be considered. It is not sufficient for there simply to be a 'significant change' in the gross value of the assets.

Tax Office access to family court material

Posted 7 October 2014

One area of the law that continues to evolve relates to the Tax Office being able to access material lodged as part of family law proceedings. A further example of this is the case of FCT & Darling [2014] FamCAFC 59. A full copy of the decision is available via the following link –

http://www.austlii.edu.au/au/cases/cth/FamCAFC/2014/59.html

Whereas the original decision prevented the Tax Office from accessing certain information disclosed by the husband in his family court affidavit, the Tax Office was ultimately given access to the material on appeal.

While the court acknowledged that they did not want to create an environment that discouraged those involved in family court proceedings from making full and frank disclosures, it was also the case that, given the family court had an inherent ability to refer matters of tax evasion to the Tax Office, any further access granted on a case by case basis was unlikely to have a significant impact.

The other specific reasons given by the court for allowing access included:

(1) there were significant restrictions on the Tax Office in relation to the ability to use the information that they gained, particularly in relation to releasing it publicly;
(2) while the husband had argued that it would be inconvenient to have the information released, there was no actual evidence supporting this argument;
(3) the Tax Office was engaged in a significant and targeted audit in relation to the husband – i.e. the Tax Office was not engaged in some form of 'fishing expedition'.

Overall, it was deemed to be in the public interest to allow the commissioner access to the material.

Next week's post will consider the Decision Impact Statement recently released by the Tax Office.

Tax Office views on accessing to family court documents

Posted 14 October 2014

As mentioned in last week's post, in the case of Darling, the Tax Office was given access to material lodged as part of family law proceedings, to further its audit activities in relation to the husband of the marriage.

The Tax Office has now released a Decision Impact Statement in relation to its intended approach in this area. As usual, a full copy of the document is available via the following link –

http://law.ato.gov.au/atolaw/view.htm?DocID=LIT/ICD/M34of2014/00001

In addition to providing a useful summary of the key aspects of the court decision, the Statement confirms –

(1) There is an implied obligation on the Tax Office not to make use of documents disclosed as part of a family law case for a purpose not related to the family court litigation (ie to assist the Tax Office with its tax audit activities).
(2) Whenever the Tax Office is wanting access to court documents for use other than in relation to the case in which the documents were filed, it will make an application to the court for release from the implied obligation.
(3) In making an application to court, the Tax Office will have regard to the factors set out in the Darling decision (as summarised in last week's post).

Tax Office denied access to family law documents

Posted 28 October 2014

Following on from recent posts, another decision arising out of family law proceedings that is worth remembering is International Litigation Partners Pte Ltd v FCT [2014] FCA 671.

If you would like a copy of the decision please email me. In this particular case, the Tax Office had sought access to material filed in the family court proceedings to assist in determining the tax residency of various related entities of the husband. While the former wife consented to access being granted, the husband opposed access.

In ultimately denying the Tax Office access to the documents requested, the court confirmed:

(1) The court must use its discretion to determine whether access to family court documents is appropriate on a case by case basis.
(2) The exercise of the discretion involves the weighing of a number of competing interests, and in particular, whether the Tax Office was likely to

derive any substantial benefit by breaching the confidential nature of personal documents filed in family court proceedings.

(3) The court should also take into account practical difficulties in separating documents that might be of use to the Tax Office and those that disclose personal issues (including those concerning the children of the relationship).

(4) Also of relevance is whether the spouse to the marriage is party to a Tax Office litigation (in this case, the husband was not a party). As set out in earlier posts, in the Darling matter, the husband was a party to Tax Office audit activity.

Family court cases and the Stamps Office

Posted 25 November 2014

Recent cases have explored various aspects of the Tax Office's ability to access material lodged as part of family law cases.

The recent family law case of Kern [2014] FCCA 1108 provides an example of where the interest of a State based revenue office can be enlivened.

If you would like a copy of the decision please email me.

The key components of the case here were as follows:

(1) A couple who had a 9-year marriage were engaged in proceedings in relation to the division of matrimonial assets.

(2) One of the assets related to some land that was gifted to the wife by her parents.

(3) Stamp duty was paid on the transfer at a value of $110,000.

(4) Evidence given by the wife to the family court was that the true market value of the land at the date it was gifted to by her parents was in the region of $150,000 and indeed, may have been closer to $200,000, particularly given that the final sale price for the land when it was subsequently disposed was $325,000.

While the family court accepted the wife's arguments that she should receive a disproportionate share of the proceeds of the sale of the land due to the contribution that she made, it was also decided to refer the evidence to the Stamps Office for further investigation.

The family court has the inherent power to make a referral in situations such as this (i.e. effectively fraud) under the *Evidence Act* 1995.

While that Act does provide some protection for self-incrimination, that protection was not available in this case because:

(1) The wife provided the incriminating evidence of her own free will.
(2) The evidence provided was done so before a request for immunity was made.

Using discretionary trusts to protect inheritances

Posted 14 April 2015

As set out in earlier posts, and with thanks to the Television Education Network, today's post addresses the issue of 'Using discretionary trusts to protect inheritances' at the following link –

https://www.youtube.com/watch?v=lkkevmdo4MU&feature=youtu.be

As usual, a transcript of the presentation for those that cannot (or choose not) to view the presentation is below –

> Historically, the reality has been that no matter if it's a normal family trust or some form of testamentary trust, there's been a general acceptance that the Family Court could attack the assets of that trust in particular circumstances.
>
> However, if it was structured appropriately, and care was taken in terms of how the trust structure was setup, then the assets of a trust would generally be quarantined. The concern in recent times has been the decision of *Spry*, which received a lot of media attention.
>
> That decision seemed to create the impression, on the face of it, that no matter what form of structure was setup – family trust or testamentary trust – and no matter how that was crafted in terms of the control structure of the arrangement, the assets of the trust would always be completely exposed. So, obviously a decision that created a radical change in terms of the way people approach setting up trust structures.

Impact of the Spry decision on trusts

Posted 21 April 2015

As set out in earlier posts, and with thanks to the Television Education Network, today's post addresses the issue of 'Impact of the Spry decision on trusts' at the following link – ***https://www.youtube.com/watch?v=mFkCvyZaqZs&feature=youtu.be***

As usual, a transcript of the presentation for those that cannot (or choose not) to view the presentation is below –

> There is no doubt that immediately following *Spry*, basically everyone was assuming that the position moving forward would be that no matter how you setup a trust, and no matter if it was a family trust or a testamentary trust, it would never provide any level of asset protection at all.
>
> However, the reality in relation to *Spry* is that a lot of the reasons for it having such a radical impact in that particular scenario were really driven by the factual circumstances of the case.
>
> For example, there were allegations, though not proven, neither were they disproven, regarding mismanagement of trust assets, deliberate threats to actually destroy trust property, and deliberate attempts to mislead the judges through the various stages of the court process.
>
> If you look at *Spry* in the context of these allegations, in terms of the wider factual scenario, and some of the subsequent cases, it's probably fair to say that you can distinguish a lot of the general trust structuring planning is in this area, away from the decision of *Spry* itself.

Lessons from decisions since Spry

Posted 28 April 2015

As set out in earlier posts, and with thanks to the Television Education Network, today's post addresses the issue of 'Lessons from decisions since Spry' at the following link – ***https://www.youtube.com/watch?v=IWsmKqpgwbs&feature=youtu.be***

As usual, a transcript of the presentation for those that cannot (or choose not) to view the presentation is below –

> Immediately following *Spry*, the feeling of many observers was that there would never be any outcome in a family law matter other than to say that the assets of trusts were entirely exposed.

What actually happened, however, is that despite the decision in *Spry* and a number of subsequent decisions have reinforced this, that trusts potentially remain a very robust asset protection vehicle.

Having said that, it is also clearly the case that the court will not be in any way restricted in terms of what they can and cannot do with the assets of a trust, if they have a legitimate reason to believe that there are grounds for doing so.

Some examples might be if:

a the trust is actually the 'alter ego' of one of the parties to the relationship;
b it can be seen that the assets of the trust have really been created because of the joint effort of the relationship; and
c the assets of the trust have traditionally always been used for the benefit of not just the two spouses, but also wider family members.

In each of those types of scenarios, the court will rely on, if not *Spry* itself, certainly principles adjacent to *Spry*, to look beyond the trust structure and deal with the underlying assets of the structure.

The 'Jodee Rich' changes

Posted 30 June 2015

As set out in earlier posts, and with thanks to the Television Education Network, today's post addresses the issue of 'The 'Jodee Rich' changes' at the following link – ***https://www.youtube.com/watch?v=8YzQI7nsYI8***

As usual, a transcript of the presentation for those that cannot (or choose not) to view the presentation is below –

The *Jodee Rich* case related to Mr Rich who was one of the directors of One.Tel.

The allegations were that almost immediately before, that is a matter of days, before it became public knowledge that One.Tel had been insolvently trading, Mr Rich took steps to transfer significant assets out of his name and put them into his spouse's name. He did that using particular provisions under the family law legislation, which at the time actually took priority over the bankruptcy laws.

As most will know, the bankruptcy legislation allows trustees in bankruptcy to clawback assets that are disposed of immediately before bankruptcy. When Mr Rich did the transfers, the family law rules allowed the bankruptcy rules to be ignored, so the creditors would have been left exposed.

In the particular factual scenario of Mr Rich's situation, he actually voluntarily agreed to unwind the transfers. However, the fact that Mr Rich had even tried to do the transfers was enough of a catalyst for the government at the time to bring in amending legislation.

The law now requires anyone that has both a relationship issue and creditors in play at the same time, for all of those parties to be heard before the same judge and for that judge to then make a decision as to how the assets should be dealt with.

Spry enforcement proceedings

Posted 11 August 2015

As set out in earlier posts, and with thanks to the Television Education Network, today's post addresses the issue of '*Spry* enforcement proceedings' at the following link – ***https://www.youtube.com/watch?v=6ewuWIpJE3g#action=share***

As usual, a transcript of the presentation for those that cannot (or choose not) to view the presentation is below –

Stephens is the case about the actual enforcement proceedings of the *Spry* case and it reinforces just how wide powers of the court are, in terms of making and implementing decisions under the property settlement regime.

In the particular case of *Stephens*, there were aspects of the judgment that saw transactions that took place after the relationship had broken down, completely ignored and unwound.

What the court also did was unwind transactions that had taken place before the relationship had broken down as well as those which related to third parties.

For example, independent trustees and the children of the relationship who had been involved in those transactions were actually forced to comply with orders, that on the face of it just applied to Dr and Mrs Spry.

Party de-identification in court decisions

Posted 18 August 2015

As a general statement, one of the key principles of the court system in Australia is that of open justice. The vast majority of cases are held in an open court, and the decisions when released, provide a full factual background and detailed analysis of the relevant legal issues.

This said, the principles of open justice do not automatically require the publication of the identity of the parties involved.

Particularly where the court believes that an individual involved in the case would be impacted on adversely in terms of their privacy and dignity, their personal details are often de-identified when the decision of the case is released.

The three primary techniques used in this regard are:

a referring to the parties by reference to initials;
b referring to the case simply by reference to a number; and
c particularly in family court cases, a protocol is often adopted where the first initial of the parties' names is used and the same number of letters are also used, however an entirely new word is created. For example, a case involving a party named 'Burgess' may instead be referred to as the case of 'Boseman'.

Lessons from the Family Court case of Essex

Posted 3 November 2015

As set out in earlier posts, and with thanks to the Television Education Network, today's post addresses the issue of 'Lessons from the Family Court case of Essex' at the following link–

https://www.youtube.com/watch?v=McHPGXipl2I

As usual, a transcript of the presentation for those that cannot (or choose not) to view the presentation is below –

While *Essex* hasn't probably received as much media attention as the *Spry* decision, in some respects, it's arguably the leading decision in the family law space in relation to trusts. As usual, a full copy of the decision is available here

http://www.austlii.edu.au/cgi-bin/sinodisp/au/cases/cth/FamCAFC/2009/236.html?stem=0&synonyms=0&query=essex.

The husband in Essex:

a was not the trustee of the structure;
b had not really received any distributions; and
c had not contributed to the assets of the trust being generated in the first place as they had come down the family line.

> Despite these facts, the court still held the assets to be the husband's resource and therefore took into broad account the terms of matrimonial property settlement.
>
> Importantly though, the assets were not considered property. That was a very important part of the decision, because the court also found that despite the fact that the husband did not have any control over the structure and had yet to receive any benefit, there was absolutely clear evidence that he would ultimately receive it, in the court's opinion.
>
> While on the face of the decision, *Essex* probably a 'loss' for the husband, the reality is that the decision supports this idea that trust structures will only be attacked where the court believes that it is absolutely legitimate in the circumstances and in any other scenario that the integrity of the trust structure will be respected and the assets will, therefore, be protected.

Are trusts still useful post *Spry*?

Posted 24 November 2015

As set out in earlier posts, and with thanks to the Television Education Network, today's post addresses the issue of 'Are trusts still useful post *Spry*?' at the following link –

> ***https://www.youtube.com/watch?v=IjcRGemWHyk***

As usual, a transcript of the presentation for those that cannot (or choose not) to view the presentation is below –

> Certainly, immediately following *Spry*, for an extended period, the usefulness of trusts was under the spotlight and there was significant nervousness about how robust they actually were going to be.
>
> The reality has been that this conclusion has been tempered by the combination of firstly the fact that *Spry* is a bit of an outlier decision and actually driven a lot by factual scenario, which is a relatively strange set of circumstances, and the fact that there have been so many cases since *Spry* that have respected the integrity of trusts.
>
> Therefore, it is generally accepted that all forms of trusts, particularly testamentary trusts, will remain the vehicle of choice in estate planning context at least for the foreseeable future.

Chapter 1(d)

ASSET PROTECTION – TRUSTS

Importance of minimising loan accounts to at risk beneficiaries

Posted 8 July 2014

As set out in earlier posts, and with thanks to the Television Education Network, today's post addresses the issue of 'Importance of minimising loan accounts to at risk beneficiaries'. If you would like a copy of the video link please email me.

As usual, a transcript of the presentation for those that cannot (or choose not) to view the presentation is below –

> The reality in relation to beneficiary loan accounts is that sometimes they're unavoidable.
>
> If distributions are being made by the trustee down to an at risk beneficiary and those amounts aren't physically paid, then they'll sit on the balance sheet either as a credit loan or an unpaid present entitlement.
>
> In either scenario, that's clearly an asset of the at risk beneficiary. So it's really important that on a regular basis those potential assets are reviewed and steps are taken to ideally quarantine them away into a protected environment.
>
> The simplest approach, assuming that you can't avoid the distributions coming down to that person, will be to forgive that debt, or as an alternative, making sure that the outstanding amount is gifted across to a protected environment whether that be a spouse, some other family member or perhaps some other related structure.
>
> The critical thing in all of that, quite aside from the pure bankruptcy issues is however that there must be a particular effort applied to the related issues. That is, things like the commercial debt forgiveness rules, wider tax planning issues and the stamp duty rules, that are unfortunately different in every jurisdiction around the country, are all potentially relevant before any step can be taken to quarantine the loan account wealth.

Is appointorship an asset?

Posted 15 July 2014

As set out in earlier posts, and with thanks to the Television Education Network, today's post addresses the issue of 'Is appointorship an asset?' If you would like a link to the video please email me.

As usual, a transcript of the presentation for those that cannot (or choose not to) view the presentation is below –

> Whether the appointor role is an asset on the holder's bankruptcy is probably one of the most contentious issues to have arisen in recent years. Certainly, the feeling amongst lawyers that act on behalf of trustees in bankruptcy or creditors is that absolutely the role is a potential asset.
>
> If it is an asset, then it forms part of the bankrupts' estate. The reality however when you actually look at the decisions that have been handed down is the exact opposite. So in other words, the role of an appointor is a personal role, akin to a directorship. Therefore, that's not an asset that can be handed onto creditors.
>
> Having said this, the issue does not seem to be going away and the conservative view would be that you would try, when setting up this type of structure, to ensure that you do one of a myriad of things.
>
> So for example, making sure that if there is an at risk person that is needing to fulfil the role of appointor or principal, that they don't fulfil that role individually and solely, that ideally there's some other person acting with them.
>
> Secondly, the way in which the role is structured, it's embedded under the trust instrument, whether it be a family trust or a testamentary discretionary trust, the appointor is automatically disqualified in the event of committing an act of bankruptcy.

Impact of Richstar on discretionary trusts

Posted 22 July 2014

As set out in earlier posts, and with thanks to the Television Education Network, today's post addresses the issue of 'Impact of Richstar on discretionary trusts'. If you would like a link to the video please email me.

As usual, a transcript of the presentation for those that cannot (or choose not) to view the presentation is below –

> Probably the most interesting part of Richstar is that in some respects counter-intuitively, it confirms that trusts remain a very robust structure from an asset protection perspective.
>
> If you actually take a helicopter view of where the court landed in Richstar, it certainly supports this idea that just because an individual happens to be the trustee

and beneficiary and appointor will not of itself mean that the trust is ignored and that the assets of the trust will automatically be deemed to be those of the relevant individual.

In contrast however, and the flipside to this argument is that if you do fulfil a number of those roles and the court feels as though that's enough in combination to create a scenario where a person is effectively the alter ego of the trust, then indeed the trust structure will not provide you any asset protection and the assets will be potentially exposed.

Scope of the Richstar decision

Posted 30 July 2014

As set out in earlier posts, and with thanks to the Television Education Network, today's post addresses the issue of 'Scope of the Richstar decision' at the following link – ***https://www.youtube.com/watch?v=N2VpKrws93c&feature=youtu.be***

As usual, a transcript of the presentation for those that cannot (or choose not) to view the presentation is below –

> It's fair to say Richstar is seen as probably the high watermark in relation to how the assets of a trust may be exposed in the context of some sort of bankruptcy litigation. Interestingly, it has remained almost as an outlier decision.
>
> There really haven't been any decisions that have supported the landing the court reached in relation to Richstar. On top of that, the cases like Smith which have come down since Richstar, effectively completely ignore Richstar and go to the extent of saying it doesn't actually represent good law.
>
> Ultimately, pragmatically and practically what the position seems to be is as long as a trust is structured appropriately it will provide a very good level of asset protection from creditors and should be seen as probably the choice structure in an estate planning exercise under a will – in other words, the use of a testamentary discretionary trust – in order to provide an adequate level of protection.

Cases that have considered Richstar

Posted 23 September 2014

As set out in many earlier posts, the Richstar case was decided in 2006, and yet, it continues to receive significant attention.

Interestingly, there has not been a substantive case that has accepted the conclusions in Richstar, and indeed, there are now many cases that have effectively rejected the core aspects of the decision in Richstar.

A selection of the subsequent cases is summarised below. If you would like access to the full copies of the decision, please email me:

(1) *Tibben & Tibben* [2013] FamCAFC 145 – The only 'entitlement' of the beneficiaries under the Deed of Settlement was a right to consideration and due administration of the trust: *Gartside v Inland Revenue Commissioners*;

(2) *Deputy Commissioner of Taxation v Ekelmans* [2013] VSC 346 – The applicant relied on the decision in Richstar to contend that the cumulative effect of the role and entitlement of Leopold Ekelmans under the trust instruments amounted to a contingent interest in all of the assets of the trust, making those assets amenable to a freezing order as if the assets of Leopold Ekelmans. The Court found that the applicant could not in this matter rely on Richstar;

(3) *Hja Holdings Pty Ltd and Ors & Act Revenue Office (Administrative Review)* [2011] ACAT 91 – notwithstanding that beneficiaries under a ... discretionary trust have some rights, such as the right to have the trust duly and properly administered, generally a beneficiary of a discretionary trust, who is at arm's length from the trustee, only has an expectancy or a mere possibility of a distribution. This is not an equitable interest which constitutes "property" as defined;

(4) *Donovan v Sheahan as Trustee of the Bankrupt Estate of Donovan* [2013] FCA 437 – a beneficiary of a non-exhaustive discretionary trust has no assignable right to demand payment of the trust fund to them (and nor have all of the beneficiaries acting collectively) and that the essential right of the individual beneficiary of a non-exhaustive discretionary trust is to compel the due administration of the trust;

(5) *Simmons and Anor & Simmons* [2008] FamCA 1088 – the court and parties referred to Richstar on a number of occasions and confirmed that a beneficiary has nothing more than an expectancy.

Chapter 2(a)

ESTATE PLANNING – TESTAMENTARY TRUSTS

Testamentary trusts – is it ever too late?

Posted 19 May 2010

As you may recall from previous posts, there are significant advantages of utilising a testamentary discretionary trust (TDT) as part of an estate planning strategy.

We often receive queries from clients asking whether it is possible to establish a TDT to receive estate assets after a person's death.

While establishing a TDT in a person's will is by far the simplest approach, it is possible for an estate proceeds trust (or post-death TDT) to be established following a person's death to receive the estate assets.

Any property received from the estate may be transferred to an estate proceeds trust (EPT) within three years for the date of death, provided the trust is structured to satisfy the requirements in the tax legislation.

A summary about EPT is available on the View Legal website (www.viewlegal.com.au) via the 'learn' and then 'resources' tabs and explains the requirements in further detail.

Practically, the area where we see the biggest demand for estate proceeds trusts is in relation to receiving insurance proceeds from life insurance policies.

Lineal descendant trusts

Posted 27 June 2011

One of the other queries that has been raised following the last couple of posts concerns lineal descendant trusts.

There are a number of names in the marketplace for this type of structure, however in very broad terms, these types of trusts involve narrowing the range of potential beneficiaries that might otherwise be expected under a family trust.

In particular, the range of beneficiaries is often limited to the direct lineal descendants of the primary beneficiaries of the trust.

As has been mentioned a number of times in earlier posts, it is always critical to read the trust deed and lineal descendant trusts are another example of this rule. One of the key issues to be mindful of in this regard is that some trusts 'reserve' only the capital for lineal descendants, while still allowing very wide distribution powers for income.

Next week, we will look at a very practical, post Bamford, implication of the lineal descendant trusts that only limit capital distributions.

What are some of the steps taken in relation to regulating control of testamentary trusts

Posted 14 May 2012

As set out in earlier posts, and with thanks to the Television Education Network, today's post addresses the issue of 'What are some of the steps taken in relation to regulating control of testamentary trusts?' at the following link –

https://www.youtube.com/watch?v=A104L8JfGGw&feature=youtu.be

As usual, a transcript of the presentation for those that cannot (or choose not) to view the presentation is below –

> The reality I think for many people in this area at the moment that estate planning as a whole, and particularly the use of more bespoke forms of testamentary trusts, is the 'new black'.
>
> What that has meant I think for a lot of advisers in this area, particularly for those with legally trained advisers is that many of the concepts that you see in wider corporate law or corporations law are now actually being filtered back into traditional estate planning.
>
> What we're finding, particularly where people are wanting to use trusts that are going to last at least 2 generations, possibly even 3 or 4, is that the regulatory regime, if you like, sitting around the control of those structures is becoming far more sophisticated.
>
> Probably the biggest thing we're seeing in that area is the use of specifically set up trustee companies. Not in terms of the government setup structure, but in terms of the actual client setting up a corporate structure and being very particular about the way the constitution of that company is crafted, the way shareholders can be nominated, the way directors are appointed and the way voting takes place within that structure all overseeing the way in which the actual trust is going to be run moving forward.

When will 'master' trusts be uncommercial?

Posted 3 September 2012

As set out in earlier posts, and with thanks to the Television Education Network, today's post addresses the issue of 'When will 'master' trusts be uncommercial?' at the following link – ***https://www.youtube.com/watch?v=9JGjM-_h2Ac&feature=youtu.be***

As usual, a transcript of the presentation for those that cannot (or choose not) to view the presentation is below –

> The issue in relation to when the traditional master trust might not in fact be entirely commercial is probably very similar to many other issues in this area in so much as there's a myriad of reasons why it might not be entirely sensible.
>
> Three common themes that I would probably encourage people to keep an eye out for would be – firstly, that the overall value of the estate just doesn't justify any form of testamentary trust.
>
> In other words, the ongoing administrative cost and the actual costs to actually set the structure up just don't make it economical, and part of it might be that because the will makers' are ultimately wanting to spend the kids' inheritance, so they're actually going to make sure that it's all gone in the first place. That would be the first category.
>
> The second category would be what we would describe as an estate where there is 'enough wealth to be dangerous' –so in other words, not wanting to put any actual numbers around it, but if there are, say, ultimately 3 or 4 children that are going to take a benefit, but the overall portfolio of the estate makes it unwise to be trying to lock that into one particular structure, and it would be in fact better for everyone concerned that they each get their own piece of the pie as it were, then that can be another big reason to sort of trend away from master trusts.
>
> That can often be driven not just by the financial numbers involved, but also practically, if you've got children spread all around the world, it may not be the absolute smartest thing to be trying to lock them into one structure.
>
> The third big reason tends to be actually at the other end of the scale where you've got significant wealth involved, serious wealth involved, and you've got the will maker sitting there and saying look, at the end of the day, while we're very happy to have the master trust as a big part of what we're trying to achieve here, we need to be able to allocate some money off directly to the ultimate beneficiaries. So that they actually can have something they can touch and feel – I guess it's called the 'beer money' trust on the side.

In those cases, it's not so much that the master trust is uncommercial overall, it's more that if you only had a master trust, that would be an unwise way to go in a particular set of circumstances.

Single v multiple testamentary trusts: The debate

Posted 19 November 2012

One issue that comes up regularly in estate planning exercises where there is more than one family unit ultimately to benefit, is whether a single or multiple testamentary discretionary trusts (**TDTs**) should be implemented.

For example, if there are three adult children, each to share an estate, should those three children jointly control a single TDT or should each child (perhaps with a co-trustee) control a separate TDT, with each TDT receiving one-third of the estate.

As with many aspects of estate planning, there is no 'correct' approach. This said, some of the factors that would tend to support using a single TDT include:

(1) if some (or all) of the children are under the age of 18 – an estate planning exercise should always be undertaken on the assumption that the willmaker dies shortly after signing the document. Therefore the primary focus should be on the needs of the surviving spouse. In these circumstances, it is generally not appropriate for the wealth to be held across multiple TDTs where the surviving spouse will likely be in control for many years;

(2) if asset protection (for example guarding against a relationship breakdown of any of the children) is critical, then generally a single TDT will be the more robust approach;

(3) if the vision of the will maker is to have the next generation (i.e. their children) effectively act as 'custodian' for future generations, then this is normally more easily achieved via a single trust; and

(4) if the underlying nature of the assets would make a 'split' ownership structure unduly complicated – for example if there is, say, one significant asset (such a property or business).

The next post will focus on some of the reasons that a multiple TDT strategy might be more appropriate.

Single v multiple testamentary trusts: The debate continues

Posted 26 November 2012

Last week's post set out a number of reasons as to why a single testamentary discretionary trust (**TDT**) might be the preferred structure, even if there are multiple family members to benefit under an estate plan.

As noted there are a number of factors that need to be taken into account in any particular estate planning exercise and there are a wide range of the factors that might be relevant in deciding to implement multiple TDTs.

Many of these factors have a practical focus and can include:

(1) the different geographical locations of the children – particularly if one or more children live overseas;
(2) poor relationships between siblings (or their respective spouses) meaning that jointly controlling wealth is likely to further fragment family dynamics;
(3) the risk profiles of each child's investment outlook;
(4) the underlying nature of the wealth – for example, if particular assets are earmarked for the sole control of a particular beneficiary;
(5) differences in the 'life cycle' of each beneficiary – for example if one child themselves has young (or no) children whereas another child has adult children, their investment objectives can look quite different;
(6) the desire to have different control mechanisms in relation to different children – for example one child might be the sole controller of their TDT whereas another child may have one or more co-trustees, or indeed, not be a trustee at all; and
(7) there can be a myriad of difficulties that arise if a single TDT is utilised and it is still running in, say, two generations time both in terms of overall management of the structure and how income and capital is ultimately allocated.

In the next post we will look at one further variation on this debate, the so called 'hybrid' approach.

Single v multiple testamentary trusts: The 'hybrid' approach

Posted 3 December 2012

Recent posts have looked at various aspects of the debate in an estate planning context of whether a single or multiple testamentary discretionary trust (**TDT**) will provide the best outcome.

As highlighted in those posts, there are a myriad of issues that should be taken into account and often the approach that best suits the client may change over time.

One mechanism that we have seen used with increasing regularity is a 'hybrid' approach. Under this model, elements of both the single and multiple testamentary trust solutions are combined.

For example:

(1) control of this 'head' trust is jointly shared amongst various family members and any nominated independent trustees;
(2) a separate TDT is also established for each child and their respective lineal descendents;
(3) a separate percentage share of the estate, or discreet assets, are then gifted to each of these 'sub' TDTs; and
(4) normally each child would control (perhaps jointly with a co-trustee) 'their' TDT. Each child would also have the ability to independently regulate succession of control for their trust.

As in any estate planning exercise the appropriateness of the hybrid approach will depend on a range of issues including the exact objectives of the client, the overall family dynamics and the nature and value of the wealth involved.

Court drafted wills

Posted 27 August 2013

One of the more fundamental developments in relation to estate planning in recent years has been the introduction in most Australian states of government legislation empowering courts to make wills on behalf of people who otherwise lack the capacity.

There have been an increasing number of cases to go through the courts in this area. The recent Queensland case of Re Matsis; Charalambous v Charalambous & Others [2012] QSC 439 is particularly interesting as it appears to be the first case that allowed a court-ordered will where the primary objective was not because the relevant incapacitated person had no will at all. Rather the situation was that the pre-existing will did not achieve the appropriate asset protection and tax planning objectives of the ultimate beneficiaries.

For those interested in reading a full copy of the decision, a link to the judgment is as follows: ***http://www.austlii.edu.au/au/cases/qld/QSC/2012/349.html***.

The case involved a businessman who had accumulated some millions of dollars of wealth and who had signed an 'interim' will, which did not incorporate any testamentary trusts, sometime before losing capacity to dementia.

On the application of the ultimate beneficiaries, the court allowed them to introduce comprehensive testamentary trust provisions into the will as if they were inserted before the will maker's death.

Next week's post will focus on some of the key aspects that the court took into account before allowing the variation to the will.

Using court drafted wills to achieve asset protection and tax planning

Posted 3 September 2013

Last week's post focused on the recent case of Re Matsis.

This recent decision was one of the first situations where a court permitted a new will to be prepared for someone who had lost capacity where the primary reason for the application was not that the person had no will.

Instead, the catalyst was that the beneficiaries were wanting to ensure the appropriate level of commercial asset protection and tax planning would be available.

The decision is particularly important because there are other cases where, in the past, similar requests have been denied.

Arguably, the important factors here included:

(1) evidence was able to be shown that the will that was in place before the will maker lost capacity was largely seen by him as an 'interim' document;

(2) the only person who could have brought a challenge against the estate was the will maker's daughter, who indicated in the proceedings that she was independently wealthy and had no intention of challenging the estate;

(3) the ultimate beneficiaries of the estate (and the people bringing the application) were the will maker's grandsons. While each of them potentially

had asset protection risks, none of them were aware of any potential litigation;

(4) the change to the existing will did not alter any of the provisions in relation to, for example, executorship or any specific gifts;

(5) while the grandsons lost direct entitlement by the inclusion of the testamentary trusts, they were still ultimately the likely potential beneficiaries via the trust structures; and

(6) the court accepted evidence that the will maker may well have himself implemented testamentary trust provisions, had he not lost capacity.

What are the exceptions to the assets of a testamentary trust being protected?

Posted 10 June 2014

As set out in earlier posts, and with thanks to the Television Education Network, today's post addresses the issue of 'What are the exceptions to the assets of a testamentary trust being protected?' at the following link –

https://www.youtube.com/watch?v=BzC3jFYyWp4&feature=youtu.be

As usual, a transcript of the presentation for those that cannot (or choose not) to view the presentation is below –

> The main exception that comes up in a practical sense is primarily for tax reasons where distributions have gone down to an at risk beneficiary out of the trust and then those amounts remain unpaid, so they become an unpaid present entitlement or they become a credit loan on the balance sheet of that trust.
>
> In that scenario, obviously, if the at risk beneficiary gets into strife and a trustee in bankruptcy is appointed, even though the asset is ultimately inside the trust, that trust has the obligation to repay the debt and the asset effectively comes out sideways in that scenario.
>
> There are however a myriad of other reasons that trusts can be at risk. Some of the obvious ones include where the at risk beneficiary fulfils a really important role in the trust, whether that be an individual trustee, a director of a corporate trustee, a shareholder of a corporate trustee, or perhaps most relevantly, where the at risk beneficiary fulfils the role of an appointor.

Segregating assets via multiple TDTs

Posted 1 July 2014

As set out in earlier posts, and with thanks to the Television Education Network, today's post addresses the issue of 'Segregating assets via multiple TDTs' at the following link – ***https://www.youtube.com/watch?v=9_dgi85kC0s&feature=youtu.be***

As usual, a transcript of the presentation for those that cannot (or choose not) to view the presentation is below –

> TDTs or testamentary discretionary trusts have historically been considered almost immune from anything in relation to wider asset protection issues, simply because they're set up under the will of the will maker.
>
> What we've seen over time however is that what has been a fairly traditional approach in terms of having very passive assets sit inside the trust has gradually expanded. It's not unusual to have business run through a testamentary trust or a partnership interest through a testamentary trust. In any of those scenarios, all of the normal principles that apply to asset protection and limited liability equally apply to testamentary discretionary trusts.
>
> As there's no extra protection provided by the testamentary trust, basic structuring issues such as utilising a corporate trustee to provide limited liability for the structure, or more importantly, ideally, using separate special purpose vehicles to undertake each uniquely risky business activity is strongly preferred.

Important considerations when establishing a TDT

Posted 9 September 2014

As set out in earlier posts, and with thanks to the Television Education Network, today's post addresses the issue of 'Important considerations when establishing a TDT' at the following link –

https://www.youtube.com/watch?v=D8HwIGVu8kk&feature=youtu.be

As usual, a transcript of the presentation for those that cannot (or choose not) to view the presentation is below –

Probably the two main components, although there's a myriad of things to be taken into account, but the two main components in light of Richstar would be firstly around control issues.

Particularly looking at things like who the trustee is of the trust, if there's going to be a corporate trustee, which is not unusual nowadays in relation to testamentary trusts, who will be the directors of the corporate trustee, who will be the shareholders of it, will there be any restrictions or prohibitions on who can fulfil those roles.

Similarly in that control context, exactly who will have ultimate control if there's going to be an appointor power? So that would be the first main category and obviously there's a range of issues that sit around that.

The second category is exactly how regulated the trust is going to be in a mechanical sense in terms of the provisions of the will. The particular things that advisers should be focusing on are issues like:

a are there automatic disqualifications for particular roles;
b if there are automatic disqualifications, do they apply permanently, or is it just during a period where a particular beneficiary or a particular appointor is in strife from creditors.

Combining these two core components and there's obviously a range of issues in between them, but generally as long as you can get those two broad silos right, that will set a good framework for a very strong structure.

Future of TDTs Post Richstar

Posted 16 September 2014

As set out in earlier posts, and with thanks to the Television Education Network, today's post addresses the issue of 'Future of TDTs Post Richstar' at the following link – ***https://www.youtube.com/watch?v=fUe8aX5DghI&feature=youtu.be***

As usual, a transcript of the presentation for those that cannot (or choose not) to view the presentation is below –

The reality is that even despite decisions such as Richstar, testamentary trusts have always been a very strong vehicle from asset protection perspective.

They're not a recent vehicle – they go right back into early English law, over hundreds of years. While there has undoubtedly been an amount of white noise around them in recent times, the reality is that they are by far and away the most robust structure from an asset protection perspective.

> Importantly, they also 'tick the box' in terms of issues such as flexibility, tax planning and overall estate and succession planning objectives can almost always be achieved via a tailored testamentary trust.
>
> Ultimately, despite the Richstar decision, it is absolutely the case that testamentary trusts remain the choice structure for most estate planning exercises.

What are superannuation proceeds trusts

Posted 30 September 2014

Recently, an adviser contacted me in relation to an estate planning exercise they were assisting with.

The lawyer advising the client recommended against establishing testamentary trusts until both the husband and wife had passed away.

The financial adviser was therefore exploring whether it would be possible to establish a 'superannuation proceeds trust' to effectively 'sidestep' the lawyer's recommendations.

For those not familiar with the superannuation proceeds trust structure, it is very similar to an estate proceeds trust (which was profiled in the post from 19 May 2010).

A summary of estate proceeds trusts is available on the View Legal website (***www.viewlegal.com.au***) via the 'learn' and then 'resources' tabs.

Structuring trusts for intergenerational transfers

Posted 25 August 2015

As set out in earlier posts, and with thanks to the Television Education Network, today's post addresses the issue of 'Structuring trusts for intergenerational transfers' at the following link – ***https://www.youtube.com/watch?v=E9Sna2eXvag***

As usual, a transcript of the presentation for those that cannot (or choose not) to view the presentation is below –

> Probably the biggest risk when structuring trusts is to look at any particular issue in isolation.

Obviously, asset protection from a family law perspective is critical and fundamental in many situations. However, it is also important to be factoring in a myriad of commercial and revenue issues, such as tax, stamp duty and GST.

There's also related issues in terms of asset protection from a bankruptcy perspective, and the overall estate and succession planning objectives.

There are a number of adjacent issues that mean whenever an arrangement is put in place, it must be reviewed regularly.

Adopting a holistic approach is absolutely critical if steps are being considered immediately before a relationship actually breaks down, because arguably the one key principle, not just out of *Spry*, but out of all the family law cases in recent times, is that the courts will look very dimly on any such steps.

When will a single testamentary trust be preferred?

Posted 29 September 2015

As set out in earlier posts, and with thanks to the Television Education Network, today's post addresses the issue of 'When will a single testamentary trust be preferred?' at the following link –

https://www.youtube.com/watch?v=-tI21UwLNnw

For ease of reference, earlier posts addressing similar issues are at the following links –

http://blog.viewlegal.com.au/2012/11/single-v-multiple-testamentary-trusts-.html
http://blog.viewlegal.com.au/2012/11/single-v-multiple-testamentary-trusts_26.html

As usual, a transcript of the presentation for those that cannot (or choose not) to view the presentation is below –

The issues around the appropriateness of a single testamentary trust structure are really driven by the practicalities and the exact factual framework that a particular client finds themselves in.

The obvious one and the most common scenario would be where the family is quite young (for example), all children who are beneficiaries are under the age of 18. Another of the reasons is if asset protection is a core goal.

Generally, the conservative view is that using one trust, as opposed to multiple trusts, will provide a stronger level of asset protection.

Other issues include where the overall framework of the people making the estate plan is one where they want to see the beneficiaries more as a custodian of wealth, as opposed to being a direct recipient.

Probably the last main example would be where the underlying assets don't lend themselves to a structure, other than being inside a single testamentary trust. A classic example would be a business interest or a large property holding. In this type of scenario, it's normally the case that a single trust would be preferred, as opposed to a multiple testamentary trust structure.

When will a multiple testamentary trust be preferred?

Posted 13 October 2015

As set out in earlier posts, and with thanks to the Television Education Network, today's post addresses the issue of 'When will a multiple testamentary trust be preferred?' at the following link –

https://www.youtube.com/watch?v=JXOrmklYY8Y

Again, for ease of reference, earlier posts addressing similar issues are at the following links -

http://blog.viewlegal.com.au/2012/11/single-v-multiple-testamentary-trusts-.html
http://blog.viewlegal.com.au/2012/11/single-v-multiple-testamentary-trusts_26.html

As usual, a transcript of the presentation for those that cannot (or choose not) to view the presentation is below –

Interestingly, the reasons supporting use of multiple trusts are almost a mirror image to those supporting a single trust. The practical reasons include where the underlying beneficiaries are all adults, spread all over the world, or simply don't get on. For any of these reasons it would often be impractical to lock them inside one structure.

Similarly, if there are different risk profiles or investment objectives for each of the underlying main beneficiaries, that would be another reason that a multiple trust would be preferable.

Again, what the underlying assets of the estate are can also be a big driver towards supporting use of multiple testamentary trusts.

For example, if there are particular assets that need to go into direct control of particular beneficiaries, then again the multiple trust structure will be the preferred approach.

Multiple trusts can be of particular use where there is a need to have different control mechanisms in relation to different components of the estate.

This can be particularly relevant to people who are concerned about the mental stability of a beneficiary or a beneficiary has a physical disability, then this in itself can be a driver to regulate part of the estate in a certain way through a testamentary trust and then have a separate trust to manage other parts of the wealth.

Chapter 2(b)

ESTATE PLANNING – TAX PLANNING

Wills post Bamford

Posted 20 June 2011

Following last week's post, there were some enquiries in relation to whether the Bamford decision meant that wills should be updated.

Very broadly, the position in relation to will updates post Bamford is similar to discretionary trust deed updates, namely:

(1) All wills should at least be reviewed (to the extent that they contain ongoing trust provisions).
(2) Our experience is that many wills probably are going to require update. The reason for this is that traditionally wills have been crafted by specialist will lawyers, as opposed to tax specialists.
(3) The significant (and very obvious) difference between trust provisions in a standard family discretionary trust and under a will, is that (in comparison) the amending of a will becomes extremely difficult following the death of the will maker.
(4) While there can be pathways to achieve an amendment after death, almost without exception it is preferable to have the will document fully in order before it comes into force.

De facto death duty confirmation

Posted 25 July 2011

As many will have seen, the lead article in Friday's Financial Review confirmed that, as far as the Tax Office is concerned, payments made by a super fund, following the death of a member, will be subject to (at least) a 10% capital gains tax bill.

Tax is payable in these circumstances on the difference between the market value of the underlying assets of the fund and the cost base.

While some advisers have tried to adopt approaches to get around what is effectively a death duty, the conservative view as to the likely ATO approach has now been confirmed beyond doubt.

Depending on the exact circumstances of a client, there are still mechanisms to significantly reduce and/or eliminate the capital gains tax liability that might otherwise be triggered on the death of a fund member, however the announcement by the Tax Office further underlines the importance of ensuring a comprehensive, integrated and up-to-date estate plan.

For those interested in reading the full draft ruling, a PDF copy is set out below. Link:

http://law.ato.gov.au/atolaw/view.htm?DocID=DTR/TR2011D3/NAT/ATO/00001&PiT=99991231235958

Do 'cascading' testamentary trusts cause a tax problem

Posted 23 April 2012

With thanks to the Television Education Network, there will be a series of posts over the next period of time where excerpts from a recent video presentation I have provided will be the basis of the post.

Each week, I will also include a transcript of the presentation for those that cannot (or choose not) to view the presentation.

The first excerpt posted today is under the title 'Do 'cascading' testamentary trusts cause a tax problem' at the following link –

https://www.youtube.com/watch?v=YaMouN6Pox0&feature=youtu.be

As explained at the above link –

Under Division 128 of the 1997 Tax Act, the concept of an asset passing from a will maker or the executor into the estate is absolutely certain that that transfer of wealth is not subject to any capital gains tax.

Where some confusion arises, particularly in relation to cascading trusts or master trusts, is that the language under Division 128 is a little bit obscure or a little bit uncertain as to exactly what is going to happen once the assets have passed into the estate.

So in other words, the transfer from the will maker to the legal personal representative, absolutely no capital gains tax.

The transfer from the legal personal representative or the executor down into an initial testamentary trust, again absolutely no capital gains tax.

The confusion then arises that is it the case that from the testamentary trust to a beneficiary, particularly if that beneficiary happens to be another testamentary trust, will that transfer be without capital gains tax?

On a plain reading of Division 128, there is little question that that transfer of subsequent assets, even if it is to another trust, will be free of capital gains tax.

There has been, for many years now, a level of uncertainty about that, simply because of the language used under that particular division.

What are the tax consequences of assets passing via a testamentary trust

Posted 1 May 2012

As set out in earlier posts, and with thanks to the Television Education Network, today's post addresses the issue of 'what are the tax consequences of assets passing via a testamentary trust ?' at the following link – ***http://youtu.be/pqngu0EddtQ***

As usual, a transcript of the presentation for those that cannot (or choose not) to view the presentation is below -

The reality has been that ever since the Practice Statement was released in around 2003, there has been a really implicit acceptance across the industry, and one would hope from the Tax Office as well, that the interpretation of Division 128 that allowed the transfer of assets, not only from a legal personal representative down into a testamentary trust, but then from that testamentary trust to another testamentary trust under some form of cascading arrangement, would be free from capital gains tax.

More importantly, any ultimate transfer out of the testamentary trust, whether it be the initial trust or a subsequent trust, would also be free of capital gains tax.

What that Practice Statement did was effectively give that approval from the Tax Office that that approach, that really had been the approach across the industry for many, many years, was not going to be challenged by the Tax Office.

What we've seen in very recent times, particularly with the 2011 federal budget, is that even though that approval seemed to be there from the Tax Office, the level of uncertainty that was created when you read that back with Division 128, meant that legislative reform was required.

We're seeing that coming through the system now with the announcement in the 2011 federal budget, which effectively looks to replicate the position under the Practice Statement from 2003.

What are the stamp duty consequences of assets passing via testamentary trusts?

Posted 9 May 2012

As set out in earlier posts, and with thanks to the Television Education Network, today's post addresses the issue of 'What are the stamp duty consequences of assets passing via testamentary trusts ?' If you would like a link to the video please let me know.

As usual, a transcript of the presentation for those that cannot (or choose not) to view the presentation is below –

One of the great difficulties in this area, and I think it's an often used phrase, is that in many respects, a lot of these issues, sort of you take one step forward and 2 or 3 steps backwards.

As much as we've touched on already, the great step forward in terms of legislative certainty around the way in which the Tax Office is going to interpret Division 128 from a capital gains tax perspective, conversely what we're seeing from a stamp duty perspective is almost the exact opposite.

So obviously, we still have a situation across Australia where every single state has different stamp duty tests and different stamp duty rules in relation to how they apply distributions under a deceased estate.

It can be said that in every jurisdiction there is certainly an alignment between Division 128 under the Tax Act for the transfer of assets from the will maker to the legal personal representative and from the legal personal representative down into a trust structure.

From there, unfortunately, it really does start to unravel quite significantly, because even in the states that historically allowed assets to be distributed out of an initial trust into a sub trust or out of an initial trust directly to an individual beneficiary, those states are starting to wind back from that position and we've got a situation for many clients where if they're going into the structure, the conservative and prudent advice will probably be that they should expect to pay stamp duty when ultimately taking assets out of the initial trust.

That line of reasoning or line of argument needs to be counterbalanced against, and the discussion about whether in fact there will be dutiable property inside the trust; and to the extent that the assets are likely to centre around cash or managed funds or shares, then it may well that for many clients the fact that there's a potential stamp duty risk down the track is in fact irrelevant.

For any adviser working in this space, the ability to give complete signoff from a tax perspective is very much counterbalanced against the fact that from a stamp duty perspective there has to be seen to be a real risk moving forward that there will be double stamp duty potentially.

Taxation Consequences of Testamentary Trust Distributions – Part I

Posted 13 May 2014

For those that do not otherwise have access to the Weekly Tax Bulletin, the article from last week by fellow View Legal Director Patrick Ellwood and I is extracted below.

In December 2013, the Federal Government announced its decision to abandon a number of proposed legislative changes in relation to various aspects of the taxation of testamentary trusts – see 2013 WTB 53 [2270] and also 2014 WTB 12 [399]. As a result, there has been a refocus on what is likely to be the approach of the ATO in this area.

Part I of this 2-part article considers the taxation aspects of:

a the transfer of assets under a deceased estate;
b distributions from a will maker to a legal personal representative (LPR);
c distributions from a LPR to a testamentary trust.

Part II of this article will focus on distributions from testamentary trusts to beneficiaries and the abandonment of the previously announced legislative changes.

Transfers of assets

On the death of a will maker, each asset of the estate will potentially be transferred 3 times:

(1) from the will maker to the LPR;
(2) from the LPR to the beneficiary of the estate, which may be the trustee of a testamentary trust; and
(3) where the recipient was the trustee of a testamentary trust, from that trustee to a beneficiary either as a capital distribution during the lifetime of the trust or as a distribution of corpus upon vesting.

The CGT consequences of each of the abovementioned transfers must be separately considered.

Distributions from will maker to LPR

The first roll-over to examine is the initial transfer of a deceased's assets from the deceased person to their LPR for distribution under the terms of the deceased's will.

As a starting point, the general position is that, when a taxpayer dies, any capital gain or loss from any event relating to a CGT asset owned by the deceased is disregarded under s 128-10 of the ITAA 1997. This means that the distribution from the deceased to their LPR does not result in a CGT liability for the deceased.

As to the consequences for the LPR, the CGT assets are taken, under s 128-15 to have been acquired by the LPR on the date the deceased died. The cost base of each CGT asset (other than for a property which was a main residence for the deceased immediately before they died) for the LPR is modified under s 128-15(4) so that:

- for pre-CGT assets in the hands of the deceased – the first element of the LPR's cost base (and reduced cost base) is the market value of the asset on the day the deceased died (meaning that pre-CGT assets in the hands of the deceased become post-CGT assets in the hands of the LPR); and
- for post-CGT assets in the hands of the deceased – the first element of the LPR's cost base (and reduced cost base) is the deceased's cost base (or reduced cost base) at the date of their death (i.e. the deceased effectively passes their cost base and reduced cost base to the LPR).

Distributions from LPR to testamentary trust

From a CGT perspective, a testamentary trust is treated much the same as other trusts. However, it should be noted that CGT event E1 does not apply to the creation of a testamentary trust since that event only applies to the creation of a trust "by declaration or settlement".

In the testamentary trust scenario, there is no such declaration of trust and there is no initial settlement sum.

The CGT rules which apply to the distribution from the deceased to the LPR apply in the same manner to subsequent distributions from the LPR to a "beneficiary" of the estate.

It would appear that "beneficiary" for the purposes of the ITAA 1997 includes the trustee of a testamentary trust (however, as will be explained in Part II of this article, for the purpose of Div 128, the trustee of a testamentary trust is also treated the same as an LPR by the ATO), meaning that distributions from an LPR to the trustee of a testamentary trust are treated in the same manner as distributions from an LPR to an individual beneficiary.

A CGT asset is taken to have passed to a beneficiary of a deceased's estate if the beneficiary (or in this case, the trustee of the testamentary trust) becomes the owner of the asset whether under the terms of:

a the deceased's will;
b under the intestacy laws; or
c under a deed of arrangement.

Section 128-15(3) provides that on a subsequent distribution from the LPR to a beneficiary (including the trustee of a testamentary trust), any capital gain or loss that the LPR makes is disregarded.

Again, the trustee of the testamentary trust is taken to have acquired the CGT assets of the deceased at the date of the deceased's death (rather than on the date they were distributed by the LPR) and the first element of the cost base (and reduced cost base) for the testamentary trust trustee will be:

- for pre-CGT assets in the hands of the deceased – the market value of the asset on the day the deceased died; and
- for post-CGT assets in the hands of the deceased – the deceased's costs base (or reduced cost base) at the date of their death.

The testamentary trust trustee is also able include in its cost base any expenditure the LPR has incurred, up to the time of the disposal by the LPR, that the LPR would have been entitled to include in its cost base had it retained the asset.

Taxation Consequences of Testamentary Trust Distributions – Part II

Posted 20 May 2014

Again for those that do not otherwise have easy access to the Weekly Tax Bulletin, Part II of the article by fellow View Legal Director Patrick Ellwood and I is extracted below.

Part I of this article (at 2014 WTB 19 [658]) considered a number of specific aspects of the transfer of assets under a deceased estate testamentary trust. Part II of the article now considers:

a distributions from testamentary trusts to beneficiaries;
b the proposed changes to CGT event K3; and
c the proposed changes where an intended beneficiary dies.

Distributions from testamentary trusts

In 2003, the ATO released PS LA 2003/12, which states that its purpose is to inform ATO staff that the Commissioner will not depart from the long-standing administrative practice of treating the trustee of a testamentary trust in the same way as a legal personal representative (LPR) is treated for the purposes of Div 128 of the ITAA 1997.

In the 2011-12 and 2012-13 Federal Budgets, it was proposed that the current ATO practice set out in PS LA 2003/12 of allowing a testamentary trust to distribute an asset of a deceased person without a capital gains tax (CGT) taxing point occurring would be codified.

While draft legislation to effect the change was prepared, the Federal Government announced that it was reviewing the progress of a large number of unenacted legislative announcements and ultimately confirmed on 14 December 2013 that the amendments would not be implemented – see 2013 WTB 53 [2270] and also 2014 WTB 12 [399].

As set out at 2014 WTB 16 [561], the ATO recently republished PS LA 2003/12 confirming that it intends to continue to consider itself bound by it. Despite the ATO apparently acknowledging that the Government will not proceed with any legislative changes, some amount of confusion has been caused by the ATO stating in updates on its website that it will "accept tax returns as lodged during the period up until the proposed law change is passed by Parliament". Those comments are contained in the ATO update entitled "Refinements to the income tax law in relation to deceased estates" (dated 22 April 2014). It is assumed these comments are simply an oversight by the ATO and that PS LA 2003/12 (as amended) will continue to be applied indefinitely into the future.

The position therefore appears to remain that there is exemption roll-over from CGT covering the "transfer" of assets from the LPR to the trustee of the testamentary trust in the first instance and the subsequent transfer by the trustee to an eventual beneficiary of the testamentary trust. The subsequent transfer may either involve a capital distribution being made by the trustee of the trust to a beneficiary during the lifetime of the trust, or a payment of capital upon vesting of the trust.

The result of PS LA 2003/12 is that, on the subsequent disposal of a CGT asset from a testamentary trust trustee to a beneficiary of the testamentary trust:

(1) any capital gain or loss that the testamentary trust trustee makes is disregarded under s 128-15(3); and
(2) the beneficiary will be taken to have acquired the CGT assets of the deceased at the date of the deceased's death (rather than on the date they were distributed by the LPR) and the first element of the cost base and reduced cost base for the beneficiary will be:
    a for pre-CGT assets in the hands of the deceased – the market value of the asset on the day the deceased died; and
    b for post-CGT assets in the hands of the deceased – the deceased's cost base (or reduced cost base) at the date of their death.

Ultimately under PS LA 2003/12, Div 128 (in particular ss 128(2), (3) and (4)) effectively applies twice:

a initially, when the LPR is the "LPR" for the purposes of Div 128 and the testamentary trust trustee is the "beneficiary"; and
b subsequently, when the testamentary trust trustee is treated as an "LPR" for the purposes of Div 128 and the beneficiaries of the testamentary trust are treated as the "beneficiaries".

CGT event K3

The ATO has indicated that the position in PS LA 2003/12 is subject to CGT event K3, which covers assets passing to tax-advantaged entities.

CGT event K3 operates to ensure that, where assets pass to concessionally taxed entities from a deceased estate, a capital gain or loss is recognised in the deceased's final tax return. This prevents assets with embedded capital gains from avoiding capital gains when they are later disposed of by the concessionally taxed entity. CGT event K3 has, in the past, been avoided by ensuring an asset does not pass to a concessionally taxed entity until after the deceased's standard amendment period (generally 4 years after the assessment) has expired.

As part of the 2011-12 Budget measures, it was announced that amendments would be made to ensure that where CGT event K3 happened outside of the deceased's standard amendment period, a CGT liability still arose in the deceased's tax return. It was proposed this could be achieved by excluding CGT event K3 from the standard amendment period.

In particular, the CGT event would have been deemed to happen to the relevant entity that passed the asset to the concessionally taxed entity (rather than with the beneficiary), avoiding the need to amend the deceased's tax return. This change would have allowed the entity to which CGT event K3 applied to be able to utilise its realised capital losses against CGT event K3, instead of the deceased utilising their capital losses against their capital gain from CGT event K3.

The change would have been consistent with how Div 128 operates under PS LA 2003/12 where an LPR or testamentary trust trustee sells an asset to a third party, rather than passing the asset to the intended beneficiary of the estate.

However, as with other proposed changes mentioned below, the announced changes to CGT event K3 were abandoned in late 2013.

Where an intended beneficiary dies before administration is completed

The Federal Government released a proposal paper "Minor amendments to the capital gains tax law" in June 2012 which specifically addressed the circumstance where an intended beneficiary dies before administration of an estate is completed. Generally, in that situation, s 128-15 provides a CGT roll-over provided that the asset passes from the first deceased's LPR to the beneficiary's LPR.

However, no CGT roll-over exists where the asset passes (ultimately) from the first deceased's LPR via the second deceased's LPR to the trustee of a testamentary trust or a beneficiary of the intended beneficiary's (i.e. the second deceased) estate because the asset was not one which the intended beneficiary owned when they died.

The former Labor Federal Government proposed to introduce measures to allow the intended beneficiary's LPR to access the roll-over where the intended beneficiary died before an asset that the first deceased owned passed to them, regardless of whether it passed first to a testamentary trust trustee. Again, however, the Coalition Government confirmed the amendments would not be implemented.

Arguably, PS LA 2003/12 can be relied on to provide relief in this type of situation.

Cascading testamentary trusts and stamp duty risks

Posted 2 September 2014

With thanks to co-director View Legal Patrick Ellwood, today's post looks at an estate planning approach that is often raised, namely the use of 'cascading' testamentary trusts. The structure usually involves a single testamentary trust being established upon the death of one spouse, which then ends and 'cascades' into multiple testamentary trusts (usually one for each child) upon the death of the surviving spouse.

This strategy is intended to avoid the issues that can arise where clients ultimately want their children to receive control of separate shares of their estate, while minimising the potential burden for their spouse with the administration of multiple trusts while they are alive.

Previous posts confirm that there should be no tax consequences of the cascading trust approach, for example see Do 'cascading' testamentary trusts cause a tax problem and Taxation consequences of testamentary trust distributions – Part II.

Although the 'cascading' trust structure can be useful in some circumstances, it is vital to consider the risk that stamp duty will normally apply on the transfer of assets from the original testamentary trust to the separate trusts for the children. The stamp duty rules are different in each jurisdiction, however will usually be around 5% of the value of the assets being transferred.

An alternative approach is to establish a single trust on the death of the first spouse, and ensure the terms of that trust are broad enough to allow capital distributions to be made to other trusts. This means that, if the stamp duty cost can otherwise be managed, the trustees can 'split' the assets of the trust into separate trusts at the appropriate juncture by way of a capital distribution.

A further alternative is to simply establish multiple testamentary trusts on the death of the first spouse and ensure the trustee of each trust (normally the surviving spouse) is empowered to administer all trusts as if they were a single trust. This approach generally provides the most flexibility and ensures there will be no unnecessary stamp duty costs.

The perceived complexities of using multiple trusts are normally not significant if the same trustee acts as trustee of each trust certainly no more complex than (say) 2 individuals owning a house, which is obviously very common.

Tax equalisation provisions

Posted 23 June 2015

One issue that comes up from time to time in estate planning exercises is the use of 'tax equalisation' provisions in wills.

Generally speaking, the approach is to seek to ensure that the after tax benefit received by each beneficiary is equal.

For a myriad of reasons, this style of clause is rarely appropriate, for example:

(1) often a client will only want to take into account the tax position in relation to a particular asset (for example, superannuation). This can lead to significant imbalances in relation to other assets in the estate – most classically, a family home which, like superannuation, can often be received tax free by a beneficiary;

(2) while there are embedded tax attributes in relation to certain assets, there can also be embedded tax attributes with the recipient – for example, if a beneficiary is a non resident at the date they receive the asset, this can trigger a completely different tax outcome as compared to a beneficiary who is an Australian resident;

(3) where assets are to pass via a testamentary trust, this can cause a wide range of potential tax differentials, many of which may be unknown for a significant period of time;

(4) similarly, to the extent that there are assets held in related entities (for example, family trusts or private companies), there may be a wide range of potential tax ramifications which again may be unknown for a significant period of time;

(5) the calculations in relation to the net position of each beneficiary can potentially be limitless – for example, additional payments made to one beneficiary to compensate for the fact that they received assets that may have a latent tax liability may themselves cause a further tax liability, which then

would trigger a further payment, which of itself would cause a further tax liability; and

(6) most clauses in this area are also crafted with reference to precise tax provisions at a particular moment in time – invariably those tax rules will have changed by the time the will actually comes into effect.

In light of the above difficulties, it is therefore normally preferable to simply set out the wishes in the memorandum of directions to the trustees of the estate to ensure that they seek specialist advice at the point of administering the will to ensure that the optimal legitimate tax outcome is achieved for the estate (and therefore the underlying beneficiaries) as a whole.

Testamentary Trusts and Excepted Trust Income

Posted 27 October 2015

For those that do not otherwise have access to theWeekly Tax Bulletin, a further recent article by fellowView LegalDirector Patrick Ellwood and me is extracted below.

The recent Tax Office Private Binding Ruling Authorisation number 1012846046513 (**Ruling**), reported in this *Bulletin*, considers a number of key issues relating to the distribution of assets via testamentary trusts under deceased estates.

The Ruling largely follows the well-publicised Practice Statement Law Administration PS LA 2003/12 (**PSLA 2003/12**), which was republished in April 2014 (reported at 2014 WTB 16 [561]), and then updated in August 2015 to the new LAPS format and style.

The Ruling is a timely reminder of the need to ensure care is taken with any intended distributions from a testamentary trust.

Overview of questions answered

The Ruling confirms the following, in each instance largely applying PSLA 2003/12:

- Div 128 of the ITAA 1997 applies to disregard any capital gains tax on the distribution of assets from a testamentary trust directly to individual beneficiaries of a testamentary trust;
- a valid variation of a testamentary trust to allow distributions to inter vivos trusts, that were not originally potential beneficiaries of the testamentary trust, would not trigger a CGT event; and

- Div 128 of the ITAA 1997 also applies to disregard any CGT on the distribution of assets from a testamentary trust directly to inter vivos beneficiaries of a testamentary trust.

Aside from also making comments about the non-application of the anti-avoidance provisions under Pt IVA of the ITAA 1936, the Ruling specifically considers whether s 102AG(2) of the ITAA 1936 would apply to treat any income derived from the assets received by an infant beneficiary via an inter vivos trust as excepted trust income.

Excepted trust income arguments

As is well understood, pursuant to Div 6AA, and in particular, s 102AG(2)(a)(i), excepted trust income is the amount which is assessable income of a trust estate that resulted from a will, codicil or court order varying a will or codicil.

The case of *The Trustee for the Estate of the late AW Furse No 5 Will Trust v FCT* (1990) 21 ATR 1123 (**Furse**) is one of the few reported decisions dealing with Div 6AA.

In that case, the Federal Court noted that provided a trust estate was created by a will, then any income of the trust estate (including a testamentary discretionary trust) is excepted trust income. The only particular limitation placed on the provisions by Justice Hill in *Furse* was that the parties must be dealing on an arm's length basis when deriving the income. Importantly, the requirement was not that the parties must in fact be arm's length but that the income was equal to an amount that would be derived had they been dealing at arm's length.

Section 102AG(1) requires that a trust have a prescribed person (relevantly in most situations, an infant, subject to certain exceptions in s 102AC(2)) as a beneficiary.

Importantly, s 102AG(1) does not expressly exclude an indirect interest as being a beneficiary for the purpose of the provisions.

Therefore, it is often argued that the income of the "trust estate" contemplated in the opening words to s 102AG(2) does not need to be the same trust estate.

This in turn means that any income received by an infant beneficiary derived from assets originally sourced from an estate, via an inter vivos trust (ie after distribution of certain assets from a testamentary trust to an inter vivos trust) should be treated as excepted trust income.

That is, the relevant income will be income that is excepted trust income "*in relation to a beneficiary of the trust estate* (that is, an inter vivos trust) *to the extent to which the amount – (a) is assessable income of a trust estate* (that is the testamentary trust) *that resulted from – (i) a will* (that is the will of the willmaker that created the testamentary trust)".

Section 102AG(4) does provide that an amount will not be treated as excepted trust income if it was derived by a trustee as a result of an agreement entered into for the purpose of securing that the income would be excepted trust income.

Arguably this restriction does not apply in the factual scenario outlined above because the income derived via the assets transferred to an inter vivos trust would have been excepted trust income in the testamentary trust.

The above arguments are largely supported by Private Ruling authorisation number 1012603789935.

Tax Office position

In rejecting the above arguments, the Tax Office confirms in the Ruling that income distributed by the inter vivos trust would not be excepted trust income.

In particular, the Ruling states as follows –

- *Furse* is authority for the proposition that excepted trust income can be sourced via a testamentary trust under a will with assets not necessarily the property of the willmaker at the date of their death;
- *Furse* is also authority for saying that inter vivos trusts can never create access to excepted trust income, unless the relevant trust is mentioned in the will; and
- this essentially means assets would need to be distributed directly under a will pursuant to a specific direction to an inter vivos trust before the income of the inter vivos trust will be considered excepted trust income.

Lessons

A number of lessons can be taken from the Ruling, including:

- The Tax Office, as has been long assumed, is likely to take a relatively narrow view to interpreting the excepted trust income rules under the ITAA 1936.
- This narrow interpretation is despite the longstanding and widely accepted principles set out by Justice Hill in *Furse*.
- Where possible, if access to excepted trust income is important to a willmaker, personally owned assets should be distributed to a trust created under a will (ie a testamentary trust), not a pre-established inter vivos trust.
- Willmakers not domiciled in South Australia looking to create a "perpetual trust" (ie set up under South Australian law to potentially avoid the need to have a vesting date) need to accept there will be risks with also accessing excepted trust income via the structure, if the Tax Office continues to look for ways to narrow the interpretation of s 102AG of the ITAA 1936 and the decision in *Furse*.
- Depending on the situation, and in particular the terms of the will, for trustees of existing testamentary trusts wanting to restructure assets and still maintain access to the excepted trust income concessions, a form of trust cloning relying on PSLA 2003/12 may be appropriate.

Chapter 2(c)

ESTATE PLANNING – GENERAL

Sole director companies – an estate planning tip

Posted 14 April 2010

During the week, due to a rather unfortunate set of circumstances, I was reminded of a very important provision under the Corporations Act.

The situation broadly was as follows:

(1) The sole director of a number of companies suddenly passed away.
(2) A number of third parties (including a financier) questioned representatives of the deceased director's estate about the authority for the company to continue to act and in particular, requested copies of the deceased's will.
(3) The deceased director in fact died without a will.

While there will be a number of issues that arise in relation to the director dying intestate (including the way in which the shares in the various companies are to be distributed amongst the family members), the immediate issue concerning who had authority to act as director of each company was resolved by a particular section of the Corporations Act

In particular there is a section that allows the legal personal representative of a sole director company to take steps to appoint a new director.

While a fairly significant amount of additional paperwork has been required because of the absence of the will, the various concerns of the financier have at least been managed for the time being.

'Same plane' provisions in wills

Posted 1 May 2010

Most estate planning lawyers recommend that every single will contain a 'calamity' provision.

This provision is also sometimes referred to as the 'same plane' clause – i.e. it is the one that applies if the will maker and all of their intended immediate beneficiaries die in the same accident.

Last week, we had a situation where the two clients (who were spouses) each had quite particular provisions that they wanted to see apply if the two of them and their children died at once. Each spouse was considering the assets they felt were 'their' assets.

Our strong recommendation was however that each spouse should in fact have mirror provisions under their respective wills and simply divide 50% of the entire estate according to each of their respective wishes.

The reason for this recommendation is that the only time a calamity provision does in fact apply is when all of the immediate family have passed away. In other words, the estate should be viewed as one combined estate and not two.

An estate planning tip

Posted 14 February 2011

Following last week's post, an adviser contacted me to relay a critical issue to keep in mind whenever looking to move an asset (such as a family home) into the name of a spouse.

Broadly the chain of events was as follows:

(1) An at-risk spouse moved the family home into her husband's name paying a substantial stamp duty bill.
(2) The husband subsequently died with a very simple 'I love you' will.
(3) Under this will, all of the husband's wealth passed back to the wife.
(4) The wife then had to pay another round of stamp duty to move the asset into a family trust.
(5) Aside from the double stamp duty bill (and the second bill was actually significantly larger than the first as duty was payable on 100% of the asset with no concessions available), the second transfer to the family trust has also meant that the house will probably be subject to capital gains tax on any subsequent disposal and the 4-year clawback period under the bankruptcy rules starts again from the date of the second transfer.
(6) Both of these outcomes could have been avoided if the husband had ensured testamentary discretionary trusts were established under his will.

When do wills need updating?

Posted 14 June 2011

In many cases, the need to update a will is obvious due to significant changes in tax or trust laws or a significant change in the circumstances for a client.

Some of the other reasons that a will may need changing are often not as obvious and a brief summary of the potential trigger points is as follows:

a there is a change of name of the will maker or anyone named in the will changes their name;
b an executor dies or becomes unwilling or unsuitable to act due to ill health, age or any other reason;
c a beneficiary dies;
d the family situation or that of any beneficiary changes (e.g. through marriage, divorce, matrimonial problems, children or further children, de facto relationships or interpersonal relationships);
e there is a material change in financial circumstances of the willmaker or any beneficiary;
f the willmaker becomes involved in a new business, company or trust.

Court drafted wills

Posted 21 November 2011

Last week, I had an example of a client situation which in some respects was similar to the post a few weeks ago where a sole director died without a will.

The situation that came up last week involved a client who was the sole director of a number of companies and had lost capacity.

While he had an attorney appointed via the Guardianship and Administrative Appeals Tribunal (there are separate entities in each state regulating how someone can be appointed as an attorney where the incapacitated individual has not otherwise made a valid appointment), the director here also did not have a will.

In many situations, there is now the possibility to apply to a court before someone's death and have the court approve a will.

The process is a relatively intense one, primarily because the court system holds the making of a will as something that in fundamental terms should only ever be made by the individual in control of the relevant assets.

This said, when compared to dying intestate, the process is often one that we strongly recommend be considered and for the client last week, we have already begun to implement the steps required to have court approval of a new will before the director dies.

How do the intestacy rules work?

Posted 28 November 2011

Following last week's post, I have had a couple of enquiries about how the intestacy rules work.

As most readers will know, the intestacy provisions apply where a person dies without a valid will in relation to all of their assets. In this regard, it can in fact be possible to die 'partially intestate'. This simply means that there are assets in a person's estate that are not validly dealt with under the will in place at a person's death.

Not dissimilar to a number of the other issues dealt with in previous posts, the intestacy rules are (at least currently) inconsistent across each state in Australia.

The intestacy rules in each state are however set out under the relevant Succession Acts and, in very broad terms, provide for the distribution of wealth amongst immediate family members according to predetermined formulas.

In very general terms, only one set of intestacy rules will apply and which rules are relevant will depend on where the deceased person was 'domiciled'.

The question of domicile can in itself a fairly complex issue and if there is a level of interest, I will try to address this in a future post.

What roles do 'quasi-ownership' arrangements play in succession planning

Posted 30 July 2012

As set out in earlier posts, and with thanks to the Television Education Network, today's post addresses the issue of 'What roles do 'quasi-ownership' arrangements play in succession planning?' at the following link – ***http://youtu.be/oUcuYyRXZ_U***

As usual, a transcript of the presentation for those that cannot (or choose not) to view the presentation is below –

This is probably a really developing area in terms of what we've seen in recent times, because out of the GFC, the changes to trust law that many of us have experienced first hand in terms of the impact of relationship breakdowns and/or the intergenerational transfer that goes wrong; you find in many family scenarios they are effectively wanting to, if not fully rule from the grave, at least do a very good impersonation of it.

In that scenario, as much as we've spoken earlier today about secured loan arrangements and actually transferring assets down and securing those under a loan arrangement; a more 'bespoke' version of that is never having the asset leave the master trust in the first place and using tools such as letters of wishes or the way in which the trustee company constitution is crafted to allow the underlying beneficiaries to have indirect access to the assets, whether they be business assets or investment assets.

Beneficiaries will probably still have to meet KPIs in relation to their performance and running of those assets, but they never actually get the physical ownership or the legal control of them.

It may be overtime that beneficiaries do ultimately receive legal ownership or legal control, but for an interim period, which may last for many years, what this final form of structure does is effectively keep the assets within the initial master trust structure and really only have a synthetic or notional allocation of assets made, at a trustee level, for the underlying beneficiaries.

Divorce and estate planning

Posted 17 June 2013

The impact of a relationship breakdown on any estate plan must be considered carefully.

While in many jurisdictions, a formal divorce leads to a partial revocation of an existing will, if the couple has only separated, or alternatively, if they have only had a property settlement, neither of these events impact on pre-existing wills.

Generally speaking, before a divorce takes place, there must be complete separation for 12 months following a breakdown of the relationship. On that basis, the conservative recommendation would be to always update wills and related documentation as soon as permanent separation takes place.

In most instances, particularly where the estate planning documents have been implemented in recent years, this process need not be time consuming nor expensive.

In an upcoming post, we will look at a client situation that arose for an adviser recently in this area.

Divorce and 'jointly' owned assets

Posted 24 June 2013

In a recent post, the impact of separation following a relationship breakdown on estate planning arrangements was considered.

One particular aspect that arose recently in this regard involved an adviser who identified that many assets owned by a couple who had recently separated were owned as joint tenants.

While the adviser was quick to ensure updated will and power of attorney documentation was put in place, at the same time, for the benefit of both spouses, steps were also taken to sever the joint tenancy ownership and convert it to tenants in common.

An earlier post summarises the distinction in this regard, and it is critical that joint ownership structures be considered as part of an estate planning review following a relationship breakdown.

The other aspect in this regard is the often forgotten requirement that before a married couple can in fact divorce, there must be evidence of an irretrievable breakdown in the relationship that has lasted more than 12 months.

As touched on in last week's post, while divorce will often partially revoke a will to the extent that it benefits a former spouse, given the 12-month 'waiting period', the conservative approach is to always update estate planning documentation as soon as it is clear that there is no real prospect of a reconciliation following the initial separation.

Temporary wills

Posted 15 July 2013

Today's post looks at a recent case in which a lawyer was successfully sued for failing to write up and sign a client's will nine days before she died (as usual, a copy of the case can be found at the following link:

http://www.caselaw.nsw.gov.au/action/PJUDG?jgmtid=164444).

The case involved a will maker (Mrs Fischer) who met with a lawyer shortly before Easter 2010 to change a gift of property she had made under her previous will in November 2009 (2009 will). Under the 2009 will, 25% of the estate passed to Mrs Fischer's son. The updated will would have distributed 50% of the estate to the son.

With Mrs Fischer's permission, the lawyer delayed preparing the new will until the week after Easter. Unfortunately, Mrs Fisher passed away before her new will was provided.

The son then claimed damages from the lawyer for the difference between the 50% he would have received and the 25% he actually received.

The Court held that the lawyer was negligent in failing to at least have an informal will signed at the initial meeting. In particular, it was held that the lawyer should have realised that although Mrs Fischer was not at a risk of imminent death, she was by reason of her age, lack of mobility and need for care susceptible to a risk of losing testamentary capacity or dying in the period of a few days between the initial meeting and the agreed date for providing the updated document.

While the lawyer was ultimately found not liable on appeal, the case remains a timely reminder of best practice in the estate planning arena.

Rights to Occupy

Posted 29 July 2013

Today's post looks at the creation of a life interest in a residential property under a will.

Traditionally, life estates were created where a will maker wanted to allow a particular beneficiary the right to reside in a property without gifting them it directly.

For a myriad of reasons, the creation of a life interest is rarely appropriate as part of a modern day estate plan, and we generally see the use of either a specially crafted testamentary trust, or alternatively, a right to occupy as the appropriate approaches to use.

Some of the reasons that life estates are no longer of particular use include:

(1) A traditional life estate is very inflexible, particularly if the life tenant no longer wishes to reside in the property.

(2) Some of the reasons that the original property may no longer be appropriate include its size, geographic location or because of the level of care required for the individual (for example, they need to move to a nursing home).

(3) Often, will makers look to craft the life estate so that it ends on the life tenant entering into a new spousal relationship – the courts have been clear that such a restriction is likely to be struck down as void.

(4) There are a number of inflexibilities in relation to the way in which the life tenant and remainderman can interrelate – ultimately, it is often very difficult to end the arrangements other than on the death of the life tenant.

(5) There are significant adverse revenue consequences, both from a tax and stamp duty perspective, that can arise in relation to life estates.

(6) The revenue difficulties are particularly detrimental if there is a desire to end the life estate before the death of the life tenant.

Signing estate planning documents

Posted 1 October 2013

We regularly review signed estate planning documentation that has been returned to us for secure storage on a daily basis.

As part of a recent quality control audit, we tracked the most regularly occurring reasons for documents being rejected for a failure to comply with the strict legal requirements in this area.

Set out below is a summary of the most common issues we identified, and it is a timely reminder for any adviser facilitating the estate planning process:

(1) attorneys signing the attorney documents before the principal has signed – an attorney can not accept their appointment before the principal has appointed them;

(2) leaving documents undated – unlike many other formal documents (for example, tax returns) where clients are specifically told not to date the document, all estate planning documentation must be dated on the day that it is signed;

(3) failing to sign (and date) in each and every place required;

(4) having witnesses who are relatives, beneficiaries or appointed in roles of authority (such as executor or attorney), all of whom are largely prohibited from being a witness;

(5) having unqualified witnesses witness attorney documents when specific qualifications are required; and

(6) attaching anything to an original document, including by way of paper clip, bulldog clip or post-it note.

If any of the above issues arise, it virtually guarantees that the relevant document must be reproduced and resigned in order to avoid substantial and unnecessary difficulties when the document ultimately needs to be relied upon.

Assessing testamentary capacity (Part I)

Posted 26 November 2013

One issue that comes up relatively regularly is the ability of a lawyer to determine whether a client has the required capacity to make a will.

Arguably, the leading case in relation to testamentary capacity dates back many years and is the decision in Banks v Goodfellow [1870] 5 LR QB 549. If you would like a full copy of the court decision please email me directly.

As set out in the decision, and as subsequently adopted and expanded on in many related cases, there are a number of key tests that a lawyer or witness to a will should consider.

The first six of these considerations are set out below (next week's post will summarise another six tests):

(1) there is no reason to consider that the person has a diagnosed condition that may affect their decision-making capacity (such as an intellectual or psychiatric disability, acquired brain injury or dementia);
(2) the person does not seem unduly forgetful of recent events;
(3) the person does not repeat themselves unduly;
(4) the person seems able to grasp new ideas;
(5) the person does not seem unduly anxious about having to make decisions; and
(6) the person does not seem unduly irritable or upset about their ability to manage tasks.

Assessing testamentary capacity (Part II)

3 December 2013

Last week's post looked at the general rules for assessing the testamentary capacity of a will maker. In particular, six of the twelve main items to consider were listed.

As promised, this week's post lists the other six main issues to consider, which are as follows:

(1) the person does not seem unduly influenced by others about their decision making;

(2) the person does not display an unreasonably low level of concern with the activities of other people (particularly their immediate family members);
(3) the person does not display an unduly low ability to adapt to change;
(4) the person did not appear to be prone to unduly losing things or themselves getting lost;
(5) there is no reason to believe the person has recently undergone a change in behaviour or experienced a change in personality; and
(6) there is no reason to believe that there are any other factors present that might indicate impaired testamentary or decision-making capacity.

In next week's post, we will consider some specific issues in relation to assessing testamentary capacity in a web-based environment.

Testamentary Capacity and web based meetings

10 December 2013

Recent posts have considered various aspects of assessing a will maker's testamentary capacity.

One issue that has come up recently is the ability for the lawyers to make the relevant assessment, where all client meetings are web-based.

Perhaps somewhat counter-intuitively, the ability to assess testamentary capacity via a web platform is often superior to the traditional, face-to-face, delivery of legal services. The reasons for this include:

(1) generally lawyers conducting a web meeting should have the general rules for assessing the testamentary capacity of a will maker top of mind at the time of conducting the web based meeting, and asks probing questions crafted to test the criteria;
(2) at View Legal, the estate planning platform via the web is a strictly wholesale platform, each client can only access the solution if their financial adviser or accountant facilitates the process;
(3) generally, any client that has an ongoing relationship with a financial adviser or accountant has a very good understanding of their financial affairs and the significance of them;
(4) the financial adviser or accountant facilitating the process will be considered by the client as their 'trusted adviser' and will often have a deep, longstanding and regular relationship with the client. Rarely do traditional law firms enjoy such a relationship with a client;

(5) as the adviser and View Legal work collaboratively, sensitive issues such as capacity of the client are far easier to raise, discuss and address;
(6) again, largely due to the collaborative approach between the adviser and View Legal, the lawyer will have received and reviewed a significant amount of detailed information about the client, which in comparison is often far more comprehensive than in the traditional process. This allows View Legal to ask far more probing and relevant questions as part of the web-based meeting;
(7) the web-based meeting is fully recorded (with the client's consent), which provides significant evidentiary advantages if ever needed, as compared to the traditional approach; and
(8) finally, the signing meeting is regularly hosted by the referring trusted adviser, who in most instances, will be best placed to very quickly identify if there has been a significant deterioration in the mental capacity of the client.

Digital Assets on Death

Posted 11 February 2014

The virtually limitless ability to create digital content has seen an increasing amount of media attention focused on ownership of content, particularly in the event of death.

In most jurisdictions, government legislation does not separately deal with digital assets, and therefore, the same rules that apply to physical assets will generally apply.

Unfortunately, many of the rules in this area lack this sophistication required to deal with digital platforms that are normally either hosted outside Australia, or alternatively, perhaps outside any discrete jurisdiction on the basis that they are cloud based.

While most digital platforms do offer deactivation mechanisms or automatic closure due to inactivity (similar to the much publicised approach taken by Google), these features do not necessarily of themselves assist in relation to ownership of the data.

Ultimately therefore, digital assets should be treated in the same way as any other asset, and to the extent that they are of significant emotive or financial value, dealt with in the last will of the owner.

Alternatively, digital assets (including passwords) should at least be communicated via documents such as letter of wishes or memorandum of directions (go to the View Legal website at ***www.viewlegal.com.au*** for a for a template memorandum of directions – via the 'learn' and then 'resources' tabs).

Some of the specific information that should be documented includes a listing of every digital platform utilised, account, user name and passwords for each platform, security question answers, and even directions as to post death activity and ultimate closure of the various accounts.

DVD Wills

Posted 3 June 2014

While not as quickly as other areas of the community, the legal industry is starting to embrace technology changes.

One case that highlights the point is Mellino v Wnuk & Ors [2013] QSC336. As usual, a link to the full decision can be found here. [***http://archive.sclqld.org.au/qjudgment/2013/QSC13-336.pdf#!***]

In summary, the critical aspects of this case are as follows:

(1) a deceased man, who had committed suicide, had made a DVD shortly before his death;
(2) on the physical copy of DVD, the man had written 'my will';
(3) the content on the DVD also, in a very informal way, explained the intention that the recording was to operate as a will on death;
(4) the court decided that each of the main requirements from a succession law perspective had been satisfied and therefore the DVD could operate as the deceased's last will;
(5) the three main tests in this regard were as follows:
(6) the DVD was considered to be a 'document';
(7) the clear intention of the document was that it articulated the deceased's testamentary intentions; and
(8) the DVD adequately dealt with all property owned by the deceased at the date of his death.

Age of majority

Posted 12 August 2014

Last week an interesting issue arose with the child of a client who was about to travel overseas on an exchange.

The child was a part time employee and member of a superannuation fund. Under the superannuation fund, they were automatically entitled to a life insurance policy which gave a payout of $200,000 on death. The fund required that any payout be made to the legal representative of a deceased member.

The parents of the child felt that it would be prudent to ensure that on receipt of these insurance proceeds the estate would be able to administer them easily – the obvious answer in this regard was the creation of a will.

Unfortunately, in these circumstances, no will is able to be made because in order to make a will, the individual involved must be 18 years of age.

The only substantive exception to this rule is if the will maker, being under the age of 18 years, has lawfully married.

Age of entitlement

Posted 19 August 2014

Following last week's post some questions were raised about at what age a person can be entitled to receive benefits under a will.

The issues in this regard are a little more complex, however broadly:

(1) If a specific entitlement under a will passes to anyone under the age of 18, the trustee of the will effectively holds it for them on a bare trust until their 18th birthday.

(2) If an age is nominated in the will for a beneficiary to receive their entitlement, it will be held on trust until that age, unless the will is not drafted correctly (there are some complex issues that can apply in this regard). If the will is not drafted correctly, then regardless of the age nominated, the beneficiary can get access to the gift on their 18th birthday.

(3) Generally, none of the above rules are applicable where the asset passes to a testamentary trust – in this instance, the assets normally remain indefinitely within the trust structure, regardless of the age of the beneficiaries.

Overseas assets and estate planning

Posted 10 November 2015

Where a will maker has assets both in Australia and overseas, there are a number of specific estate planning steps that should be adopted.

In summary, these include:

a It is generally preferable to commence the estate planning process in the jurisdiction that the will maker is currently living.

b The completed estate planning documents should be signed in the normal way and then provided to a specialist adviser in any other jurisdiction where substantial assets are held.
c While initially the will first prepared should apply to all assets worldwide, generally when documentation is implemented in other jurisdictions, each will should be amended so as to only apply to assets in the relevant jurisdiction.\
d Wherever possible, the signing and witnessing procedure for the jurisdiction to which the will applies should be followed. Alternatively, it will generally be permissible for the will to be signed and witnessed in accordance with the laws of the country where the will maker signs the document and still be valid worldwide.

The above approach ultimately ensures that the client has:

a appropriate estate planning documents for each Country in which they retain wealth; and
b received the necessary succession and tax advice for each asset in each Country.

What happens to assets in the estate if a person dies without a will?

Posted 1 December 2015

A previous post has looked at what happens to assets in the estate if a person dies without a will (see – ***http://blog.viewlegal.com.au/2011/11/how-do-intestacy-rules-work.html***).

If a person dies without a will, the law says that their assets will be distributed to their family, as determined by a set formula (the 'intestacy' rules). The set formula is different in every Australian jurisdiction. There are a range of issues which will determine which jurisdiction's rules will apply.

The intestacy rules will also apply where a person dies without a valid will in relation to all of their assets. In this regard, it can in fact be possible to die 'partially intestate'. This simply means that there are assets in a person's estate that are not validly dealt with under the will in place at a person's death.

The following summary gives a broad example of the way in which the intestacy rules often work. If a person dies leaving:

(1) their spouse, but no children: their spouse receives everything;
(2) their spouse and children: their spouse receives the first $150,000 and one half of the balance of the estate if there is one child, or one third of the balance if there is more than one child. The Testator's children share the balance between them;
(3) children but no spouse: their children receive a share each, but only if 18 years of age or married;
(4) no spouse or children: the person's parents will share the estate (if both are alive then equally);
(5) no spouse, no children and no parents: their siblings share equally.

A spouse includes a legal and de facto spouse.

The amount received by each person will depend on the value of the estate and whether any other beneficiaries are entitled to the assets of the testator.

If the person does not have any family members who qualify, then the assets may pass to the government.

It is necessary that someone apply to the court to be appointed as the administrator, to ensure that the person's estate is properly administered. This normally adds time and significant extra costs to the administration of the estate.

If the testator has young children and a guardian is needed, an application to the court may also have to be made.

Chapter2(d)

ESTATE PLANNING – CHALLENGES

Notional estates

Posted 24 February 2015

Laws in each state of Australia allow a family member or certain other dependants to challenge a deceased's will. Such a claim is generally known as ether a family provision application or a testator's family maintenance (**TFM**) claim. Whether a TFM claim is successful depends upon a range of matters – regardless of the outcome however, TFMs can be costly and emotionally debilitating for all parties involved.

Historically in all Australian states, a TFM claim could only relate to property that was owned by the deceased on the date of their death, putting certain property – such as trust assets or those owned by a spouse – outside the reach of a TFM claim.

In 2005, NSW introduced 'notional estate' provisions, which essentially enable a court to treat certain property that is not legally part of a deceased estate, as being deemed to be included and thereby open to attack by a TFM. These provisions apply to NSW domiciled persons and any property located within NSW.

For property to be part of a notional estate, 'a relevant property transaction' must have occurred, which in broad terms requires a positive act or omission that results in property being owned by someone other than the deceased. The offending transaction must have taken place within certain specified times before the date of death of the will maker.

All Australian states have been considering adopting similar notional estate provisions to NSW. The only other state to announce their likely approach has been Victoria. In October 2013, the Victorian Law Reform Commission (**VLRC**) released its final report on Victoria's succession laws, and recommended that the NSW notional estate provisions should not be adopted in Victoria.

This said, even otherwise where a state's succession laws do not include notional estate provisions, there may still be means to attack assets not otherwise forming part of a deceased's estate, including because of poor planning or due to sham, contrived or artificial transactions.

How to avoid a $25 million challenge against your estate

Posted 3 March 2015

Last week's post looked at the way in which the notional estate rules work in New South Wales. Some comments were also made about the fact that no other Australian estate has adopted, to this point, similar provisions.

During the week, the Wright estate case has received a significant amount of media attention. The decision itself is Mead v Lemon [2015] WASC 71, and as usual, a link to the decision is as follows –

http://decisions.justice.wa.gov.au/supreme/supdcsn.nsf/PDFJudgments-WebVw/2015WASC0071/%24FILE/2015WASC0071.pdf

Much of the decision has focused on the fact that the claimant, in receiving an award of $25 million has, by some $22 million, exceeded the previous largest successful application under the family provision rules in Australia.

In the context of the notional estate provisions, perhaps one of the most interesting aspects of the judgment however relates to the comments about the fact that the duty imposed under the law to properly provide for certain people is (in all states other than New South Wales) able to be avoided.

In particular, the court held –

(1) The deceased must have been aware of that duty – he was well advised by a competent solicitor. But it is a duty he could have avoided.

(2) The deceased was aware some six months before his death he was afflicted by terminal cancer. At that stage he was free to distribute his estate in any way he wished.

(3) That would have meant on his death neither the plaintiff nor anyone else could have maintained a claim – there would have been nothing to claim against.

(4) But of course if the deceased had taken that course he would have been liable for millions of dollars in, effectively, gift duty.

(5) The price the deceased paid for passing his assets tax free to his nominated beneficiaries was acceptance of the statutory duty arising to the plaintiff.

The bluntness of the above comments are a common theme throughout the judgment, and one of the quotes that has been circulated to me from multiple sources in this regard is as follows –

'The plaintiff did say she had a boyfriend whom she hoped to marry within the next two years. She anticipated having four children. Of course it is possible after one child she might reconsider; most sensible people do.'

Beyond death do us part – pre-nups and challenges against estates

Posted 10 March 2015

Following the posts over recent weeks relating to challenges against deceased estates, this week's post, with thanks to team member Hayden Dunnett, considers another relevant decision, namely Hills *v Chalk & Ors (as executors of the estate of Chalk (deceased)) [2008] QCA 159*. The case is important because it starkly highlights the potential significance of a Binding Financial Agreement (**BFA**) even where the BFA does not comply with the Family Law Act.

As usual, a full copy of the decision is available via the following link –

http://www.austlii.edu.au/au/cases/qld/QCA/2008/159.html.

Mr Hills and Mrs Chalk entered into a 'pre-nuptial' agreement in 1994, which was before the ability to make an enforceable BFA. The terms of the pre-nuptial agreement were essentially contractually based and provided that in the event of their separation, they were each to retain their own assets and make no claim for property settlement, or maintenance from the other.

The agreement also recorded a joint intention to preserve their assets for their respective families. Importantly, they acknowledged that each party should not seek to defeat the intention of the other.

Mrs Chalk died in February 2003, and probate was granted in April 2003 to the children of Mrs Chalk. In September 2007, some 4 years after her death, Mr Hills made an application for further provision from the deceased estate. In her will, Mrs Chalk had given Mr Hills a right to reside in her house, and a legacy of $20,000 in recognition of him caring for her during illness. The balance of her estate was left to her children.

The court refused Mr Hills' application stating it was 'distinctly improbable' that Mrs Chalk had failed to make adequate provision for Mr Hills.

In particular, it was held that the 'pre-nuptial' agreement made by the parties, although not of itself directly decisive against Mr Hills' claim, was of significance to the assessment to be made by the court of Mr Hills' application for further provision.

Following the decision in this case it is generally accepted that a BFA, perhaps even if not binding for Family Law purposes, will be taken into account in any claim for further provision from an estate.

When will an inheritance be at risk?

Posted 31 March 2015

As set out in earlier posts, and with thanks to the Television Education Network, today's post addresses the issue of 'When will an inheritance be at risk?' at the following link – *https://www.youtube.com/watch?v=Ks2GvSVp07U&feature=youtu.be*

As usual, a transcript of the presentation for those that cannot (or choose not) to view the presentation is below –

> There is a true continuum in terms of the approach that the court is going to take, where at one end, assets of a trust will be completely exposed and will be considered property of the relationship. At the other end, you've got a situation where the assets will be completely ignored and they won't even be considered a financial resource.
>
> Inheritance is a classic example, because in order for the court to make a decision that they're not taken into account, it really does come back, and this will often be used by the lawyers, to the two word answer – 'it depends', because it really does depend on the underlying factual matrix.
>
> If people are particularly concerned about trying to exclude inheritances, the types of things that the courts will normally gravitate towards are things like ensuring that the assets pass as late as possible in terms of when the relationship has broken down, and ideally to the extent this can ever be achieved, that the assets don't pass until after the relationship has ended.
>
> The other things that are relevant include whether the former spouse has in any way contributed to the growth of the assets that are coming via the inheritance. Obviously, and most relevantly in the context of trust planning, whether the people that are handing the assets on have done so directly in the name of the spouse, or preferably have they used some sort of trust structure – for example, a testamentary discretionary trust.

Chapter 3(a)

TRUSTS – TAX PLANNING

Pre CGT assets owned by family trust

Posted 1 April 2010

Over the last eighteen months, we have had an increasing number of clients needing to consider various aspects of the capital gains tax (CGT) rules as they relate to assets acquired pre CGT (i.e. before September 1985).

Someone like Bernard Salt (Salt is a renowned demographic consultant out of KPMG in Melbourne – ***http://www.bernardsalt.com.au/***) would undoubtedly be able to explain that the reason for this has something to do with the baby boomer generation – i.e. people who were in the early to mid part of their wealth creation in the 1980s are now looking at retirement and succession issues.

Two of the more complex aspects of the CGT regime, relate to the deeming provisions under Division 149 (formerly section 160ZZS) and CGT event K6 (formerly section 160ZZT).

As an accountant reminded me last week, there is an old ATO ruling (let me know if you want a copy of it) that confirms Division 149 can in fact apply to discretionary trusts – i.e. the underlying CGT status of trust assets can be impacted on by the way in which distributions have been made out of the trust over the term that the asset was owned.

Trust cloning is dead (or is it?)

Posted 12 April 2010

Yesterday, a suburban lawyer and I caught up in relation to reviewing a purported trust clone.

As many of you will know, we have been fortunate (particularly in recent years) to do an ever increasing amount of work with suburban and regional lawyers who effectively use us as their external resource in areas where they do not have the time, energy or skills to otherwise assist.

Here the initial query was for the lawyer directly and in particular whether he had prepared documents for a client that satisfied the relevant trust law rules about how a trust cloning must take place. As it turned out, everything was fine on this point and similarly from a tax perspective, the transaction had been validly implemented prior to the tax rule changes on October 31, 2008.

What had not been resolved however was the way in which the transfer of assets between the two trusts was accounted for. In particular, the lawyer had crafted the documentation so that the consideration paid was the amount notified to the parties by the accountant.

As no notification had yet been made, we caught up with the accountant and quickly determined that there could be four possible alternatives, namely:

(1) Nil.
(2) $1 (or some other nominal amount greater than nil).
(3) The historical cost base.
(4) The market value.

Each of these four alternatives had quite dramatically different consequences both from an accounting and tax perspective and yesterday's meeting was a timely reminder of the need for a truly collaborative approach between the various professional specialists on behalf of the underlying client.

Stamp duty and corporate trustees

Posted 7 June 2010

In recent weeks, I have touched on the difficulties that can be caused by the different stamp duty rules in each state around Australia.

Unfortunately, similar issues arise in relation to enduring powers of attorney and guardianship provisions.

Each state has a different regulatory approach in this area. While there are rules that provide that each jurisdiction needs to permit attorneys acting under a document produced in a different state, practically issues will often arise.

One example is in Queensland where one document (sometimes running to over 20 pages) can be used to appoint both attorneys and guardians. In contrast New South Wales, two separate documents (each only running to a couple of pages) are required and in Victoria, three separate documents are necessary.

Where you have clients who regularly do business in different states, it can often be of a significant practical benefit (and a large time and cost saving) to have documents prepared in accordance with each state's rules.

If your client is going to do this, you should ensure that the documents are crafted so that each one acknowledges the existence of a similar document in a different jurisdiction.

Corporate trustee duty (part 2)

Posted 15 June 2010

Last week, I mentioned the unique way in which the Queensland stamp duty rules can operate in relation to the transfer of shares in companies that act as trustees for discretionary trusts.

As touched on last week, the provisions are such that the transfer of shares in these companies can be charged with standard stamp duty rates based on the underlying market value (ignoring any debt) of the dutiable assets in the discretionary trust located in Queensland or Western Australia.

In Queensland there is however the ability to legitimately avoid this stamp duty cost, if the transaction comes within an exemption set out under the stamp duty rules.

Broadly these rules provide that so long as the transfer of shares is between individual members of a family group, and the trust is established primarily for the benefit of members of that family, then there will be no duty payable.

As the ability to access the stamp duty relief is subject to the discretion of the Stamps Office, there is the ability to get an indication on whether stamp duty relief is likely to be available and with the client that I mentioned last week, we have submitted a ruling application on their behalf.

If an unfavourable ruling is received, we will need to explore other, less commercially appropriate, alternatives to achieve the client's overall objectives.

Lineal descendant trusts

Posted 11 October 2010

'Lineal descendant trusts' come in many shapes and forms.

Undeniably, the popularity of the structure has been significant not only in recent years, but right back to the establishment of trusts as an asset protection and tax planning vehicle in early English law.

Whenever considering the establishment of such a trust (or reviewing a pre-existing trust), it is critical to understand how the legal firm involved in crafting the document has approached the task.

Some common themes for the structure of this kind of trust include:

(1) Providing that income distributions can be fully discretionary amongst both lineal and non lineal descendants, with capital only able to be distributed to lineal descendants.

(2) Both income and capital distributions being limited to lineal descendants.
(3) Income and capital distributions limited to lineal descendants, unless otherwise approved by, say, the appointor.

Complete unity in relation to tax reform for trusts

Posted 25 October 2010

Many of you will have seen the announcement last week that each of the major taxation professional bodies have called on proper reform to the taxation of trusts.

Undoubtedly, the ongoing angst caused by the ATO's approach on UPEs has been a significant part of the catalyst for this, however the reality is that the piecemeal approach to taxation of trusts has been a longstanding problem.

A full copy of the press release providing more context in this regard is set out below.

Four of Australia's leading professional tax and accounting bodies, representing over 100,000 accountants and tax advisers, have united to call for sweeping reforms of the antiquated laws governing the taxation of trusts.

In 2009 the ATO introduced a controversial crackdown on "unpaid present entitlements" –distributions by trusts to associated private companies that were not paid, but remained intermingled with other funds of the trust.

The professional bodies believe the Tax Commissioner's technical interpretation of the taxation laws (Division 7A of the Income Tax Assessment Act 1936) that apply to unpaid present entitlements is not supportable and is at odds with the original policy intent.

While the practice statement on unpaid present entitlements released by the ATO last week embraced some of the practical recommendations put forward by the professional bodies, the fundamental incorrectness of the ATO interpretation remains. This will increase the cost of a major source of financing typically employed in the SME market.

The professional bodies have called for an urgent test case to challenge the Tax Commissioner's interpretation of the laws that apply to unpaid present entitlements, and will raise the issue again at a meeting today in Canberra of the ATO's peak external stakeholder forum, the National Tax Liaison Group.

The recommendation is for the test case to be heard by the Federal Court and funded under the ATO's test case funding program, to provide judicial guidance on whether the Commissioner's position on this important aspect of the law is correct. The Tax Commissioner has accepted the proposition that a test case is an appropriate vehicle through which to resolve this issue.

The unpaid present entitlement issue, alongside a High Court decision earlier this year on the taxation of trust income and distributions, highlights the need for major review into the taxation of trusts. The Henry tax review, along with recommendations made recently in Treasury's "Red Book," both indicate that the government should re-write the trust laws which are more than 50 years old and are not adequate to deal with the modern use of trusts as trading and investment vehicles.

Institute of Chartered Accountants in Australia National Institute of Accountants Taxation Institute Taxpayers Australia

Unpaid present entitlement warning

Posted 9 December 2010

There can be a number of traps in relation to the provisions of a trust deed in the context of the Tax Office's approach in relation to unpaid present entitlements (UPEs).

Arguably, the most concerning trust deed provision that we have seen in recent times is a clause in the deed of one provider that on a plain reading of the deed seems to automatically cause any UPE to become a loan at call.

Obviously, this provision can have significantly adverse consequences, particularly for those clients wishing to 'quarantine' UPEs that existed as at 16 December 2009.

Colonial decision released

Posted 31 January 2011

Earlier in the month the long awaited 'Colonial' decision was released by the Federal Court.

Although, unlike other tax cases last year (such as Bamford and Thomas), the taxpayer was largely unsuccessful, the Colonial decision again reinforces that the provisions of the trust deed are critical.

For those interested the full title of the case is 'Colonial First State Investments Limited v Commissioner of Taxation [2011] FCA 16' (Federal Court of Australia, Stone J, 18 January 2011).

In brief terms, the key aspects of the decision were as follows:

(1) The main interest in the decision will be for the Australian funds management industry as it focussed on the tax effect of provisions in a unit trust that sort to allocate part of the taxable income to a unitholder redeeming units.

(2) The tests that must be satisfied to meet the definition of a 'fixed trust' for tax purposes will be difficult for many unit trusts.

(3) Here the unit trust was held not to constitute a fixed trust, primarily due to the wide amendment power that allowed changes to be made to unitholders' entitlements. The ability to satisfy the Tax Act definition of fixed trust is important in a number of areas including –

   a to carry forward tax losses;
   b passing through franking credits to unit holders; and
   c where superannuation funds are unitholders, avoiding application of the 'non-arm's length income' rules (note that prior to 1 July 2007, these rules were called 'special income').

(4) The attempt by way of variation to provide the trustee the discretion to allocate discounted and non-discounted capital gains to unitholders on redemption was ineffective.

As set out in the post on 17 December 2010, it has been confirmed that there will be a full review of the way in which trusts are taxed.

The Colonial decision further highlights the need for a comprehensive review of the existing rules and Stone J mentions the need for legislative change in this regard.

A number of commentators also believe the proposed managed investment trust attribution regime (due to take effect on 1 July 2011) may address many of the concerns raised in Colonial.

Trust resettlements

Posted 7 February 2011

Following on from last week's post concerning the long awaited 'Colonial' decision, another decision released by the Federal Court in the last couple of weeks is of significant interest.

In a similar vein to the high profile tax cases last year of Bamford and Thomas, the taxpayer here was largely successful.

For those interested the full title of the case is – FCT v Clark [2011] FCAFC 5 (Full Federal Court; Dowsett, Edmonds and Gordon; 21 January 2011).

In brief terms, the key aspects of the decision (which was given by way of a 2 to 1 majority) were as follows:

(1) What is required to constitute a resettlement (i.e. the disposal and reacquisition, for tax purposes, of all assets of a trust at market value) is significantly more than what the Tax Office has traditionally suggested, and indeed argued in this case;
(2) The High Court decision of Commercial Nominees confirms that to avoid a resettlement occurring, there only needs to be a continuum of property and membership, that can be identified at any time, even if different from time to time;
(3) The Commercial Nominees case, while it related to a superannuation fund, is relevant in relation to trusts more generally;
(4) In the circumstances of this case the fact that there had been a change of trustee, a change of control of the trust, a change in the trust assets and a change in the unitholders of the trust between 2 income years did not trigger a resettlement; and
(5) Where a trust has been effectively deprived of all assets and then 're-endowed', a resettlement will probably occur.

Important stamp duty changes in Queensland

Posted 4 April 2011

For those advisers who provide guidance to trusts with assets in Queensland, relatively important changes have been announced to the Duties Act.

Previous posts have mentioned the difficulties surrounding corporate trustee duty, particularly in relation to the Commissioner's discretion in determining whether it applies.

This discretion has now been removed.

Similarly, the discretion surrounding whether a trust is a 'family trust' and therefore able to get access to various concessionary provisions has also been removed.

At least on the face of the new provisions, it should be easier to implement rearrangements of family trusts (particularly in succession situations), however due to the vagrancies of how many trust deeds are drafted, advisers will need to be extremely careful to ensure that any particular change does in fact comply with new rules.

It should be noted that the changes are only in bill form at this stage – in other words, they are not formally legislated as yet.

Government review of trusts – the journey continues

Posted 11 April 2011

As most will know, the ongoing saga in relation to the taxation of trusts took another turn last week with Bill Shorten retracting his previous promise to ensure that post Bamford amendments would be implemented before 30 June 2011.

The government has now indicated that other than in relation to the streaming of income all other issues will not be considered further until the wider taxation review scheduled for October. This review has already been postponed once.

Practically the latest announcement may cause trust advisers to proceed with 'core' amendments (for example, ensuring that trustee minutes can be made after the end of a financial year) to trust deeds before 30 June 2011.

Two other important issues to note from last week in relation to trusts are that:

(1) it now appears unlikely that there will be any change to the unpaid present entitlement rules released by the Tax Office before 30 June 2011.
(2) the announcement that the Coalition will look to re-invigorate entity taxation (i.e. taxing trusts as companies) if they win the next election.

Statement of principles to be (finally) amended (?)

Posted 5 December 2011

Many readers will be aware of the full Federal Court decision earlier this year of Clark.

In that case, the Court largely reiterated the decision from 10 years ago in Commercial Nominees that, generally speaking, a resettlement of a trust for tax purposes can only happen in a very limited range of circumstances.

At the end of last week, the Tax Office released a decision impact statement in relation to the Clark decision and has, finally, accepted that the position set out in the case may mean that the 'Creation of a New Trust – Statement of Principles' last updated in August 2001, may need to be changed.

A previous post links the Statement of Principles for those that have not seen it, and in that document, the Tax Office suggests that there are in fact quite a large range of situations where a trust may be resettled for tax purposes.

It is hoped that the Tax Office can prioritise providing some clarity around their position on trust resettlements, particularly given that most specialist advisers in this area believe that, in accordance with Commercial Nominees and Clark, significant changes should be able to be made to trust deeds without triggering a resettlement.

For those interested in reviewing the complete decision impact statement, the relevant link is as follows –

https://www.ato.gov.au/law/view/document?docid=%22LIT%2FICD%2FQUD1of2010%2F00001%22

ATO releases draft determination on trust resettlements

Posted 22 June 2012

Posts from last year looked at the Clark decision. In that case, the court held that significant changes to a trust instrument would not of themselves cause a resettlement of the trust for tax purposes.

As mentioned in last week's post, the Tax Office has now released draft determination TD2012/D4 which provides some further clarity around when the Tax Office will deem changes to a trust to amount to a capital gains tax event under CGT events E1 and E2 (i.e. a resettlement).

In broad terms, the Tax Office states that unless variations cause a trust to terminate, then there will be no resettlement for tax purposes.

A number of examples are provided, which give some guidance around issues such as changes of beneficiaries and update to address distribution of trust income.

Unfortunately, the examples provided are not particularly comprehensive and issues such as changing appointors and multiple changes (for example, changing beneficiaries, the trustee and the appointor as part of an estate planning exercise) are not specifically addressed.

This said, the draft determination should provide a level of confidence that relatively significant changes to trust instruments can be made without adverse tax consequences, although it remains necessary to also consider the separate stamp duty and trust law implications of any such change.

A full copy of the draft determination is at the following link –

https://www.ato.gov.au/law/view/document?docid=%22DXT%2FTD-2012D4%2FNAT%2FATO%2F00001%22

More comments on ATO resettlements determination

Posted 2 July 2012

As mentioned in the last post, the ATO has released a draft determination, TD2012/D4, in relation to resettlements.

With particular thanks to co View Legal director Tara Lucke, today's post focuses on the interplay of the draft determination with the ATO's previous published position on resettlements – the Statement of Principles.

In summary, according to the determination:

(1) The ATO has withdrawn its Statement of Principles as of April 2012.
(2) The ATO accepts that although the Clark and Commercial Nominee cases were decided in perhaps slightly different contexts to many of the issues dealt with in the Statement of Principles, the conclusions reached in each of those two cases do have a broader application.
(3) Provided an amendment to a trust is valid at trust law and is in accordance with the terms of the trust instrument, CGT event E1 should not be triggered.

The ATO will expect any deed of variation to be made in accordance with trust law principles and the particular requirements of the trust instrument in order for the amendment to be effective.

Division 6AA and child maintenance trusts: there are advantages, but pitfalls too

Posted 24 March 2015

For those that do not otherwise have access to theWeekly Tax Bulletin, the article from earlier this month by fellowView LegalDirector Patrick Ellwood and me is extracted below.

In the context of deceased estates (and specifically with the use of testamentary trusts), the excepted trust income rules under Div 6AA of the ITAA 1936 are well known.

In particular, the rules allow income derived by infant children via distributions from a testamentary trust to be assessed at the normal, individual adult rates. As a result, the first $24,000 (approximately) is tax-free and the balance is taxed at the adult marginal rates. For most families, this can mean significant tax planning opportunities.

In the vast majority of cases, access to the excepted trust income concessions is only available following someone's death. One key structure that falls outside this general position however is a 'child maintenance trust' (**CMT**).

A CMT is another form of trust contemplated by Div 6AA that should be at least considered whenever there is a personal relationship (referred to as a 'family') breakdown and either party is responsible for making child support payments. This is because a validly established CMT can also create access to the excepted trust income provisions and the resulting tax concessions.

Given the significant percentage of personal relationships that breakdown irretrievably, many of which then result in child maintenance obligations being imposed, it is important that practitioners are aware of the planning opportunities afforded by CMTs.

What is a 'family breakdown'?

Section 102AGA of the ITAA 1936 defines a transfer of property as a result of a 'family breakdown' to include legal obligations arising from a range of situations such as:

a The breakdown of a formal marriage.
b The breakdown of a de facto relationship.
c Where a child has been born outside a 'traditional' relationship arrangement (for example, a 'one night stand').

CMTs are potentially available in relation to children who are:

a born of the union of the relationship that has broken down;
b adopted children; and
c step-children.

ITAA 1936 and excepted trust income

CMTs are specifically provided for in s 102AG of the ITAA 1936. As noted above, the main advantage of a CMT from a tax perspective is the ability for income of the trust to be treated as excepted trust income.

A CMT, like most trusts, must be established by deed but, in contrast to many of the other types of trusts contemplated by the excepted trust income rules, cannot be created by a will.

There are also other requirements that must be met before the income of the trust is treated as excepted trust income, including:

a the children named as the "primary beneficiaries" of the trust must be younger than 18 at the time the trust is established;
b income must be derived by the investment of property transferred to the trustee of the trust for the benefit of the primary beneficiary/beneficiaries, as a result of a "family breakdown", as set out above;
c there is no set time frame in which a CMT must be established following the family breakdown, although they should ideally be set up at the time of the property settlement; and
d the children for whose benefit the trust is established must ultimately receive all of the capital from the trust in equal shares.

Both in relation to tax planning and asset control, it is important to note that potential income beneficiaries of a CMT may include persons other than children of the relationship subject to the family breakdown, without jeopardising access to the excepted trust income concessions.

Non-arm's length arrangements

The income of a CMT can be generated from non-arm's length arrangements. However, any income which results from non-arm's length transactions must be of equal value to that which would have been derived on an arm's length basis in order to be considered excepted trust income.

The arm's length requirement is set out in detail in s 102AG(3). In particular, this section provides that if any 2 or more parties to:

(1) the derivation of excepted trust income; or
(2) any act or transaction directly or indirectly connected with the derivation of that excepted trust income,

were not dealing with each other at arm's length, then the excepted trust income (if any) is only so much of that income as would have been derived if they had been dealing with each other at arm's length.

Due to the strict requirements for a valid CMT, particularly on the ultimate vesting of the assets in the children of the relationship that had a family breakdown, one approach often used is to contribute depreciating assets such as plant, equipment and motor vehicles to the trust. These assets can be leased, either to a related individual or business entity for value.

Provided the lease repayments are on an arm's length basis, then the income will be able to be distributed to infant children as excepted trust income.

Other issues to consider

While there can be tax planning advantages to utilising a CMT, there are also a number of potential pitfalls (in addition to the matters set out above).Some of the things to specifically consider before establishing a CMT include:

(1) Taxation Ruling TR 98/4 which sets out in detail the Commissioner's position in relation to CMTs and should be studied carefully before implementing the structure.
(2) The CGT relief afforded by Div 126-A of the ITAA 1997 due to a marriage breakdown does not extend to assets transferred to a CMT.
(3) Similarly, in relation to non-capital assets (eg depreciating assets), there will generally be no roll-over relief available for asset transfers to the CMT.
(4) Generally there will also be no stamp duty relief available for dutiable assets transferred to a CMT, although anecdotally it appears some State Revenue Offices do allow an exemption.
(5) It is often extremely difficult to establish a CMT unless both parents work collaboratively, which obviously may not be the case where the personal relationship has otherwise broken down.

Chapter 3(b)

TRUSTS – DISTRIBUTIONS

Bamford – What exactly does it mean?

Posted 19 April 2010

One very practical issue that has been raised regularly over the last few weeks has been in relation to trust deeds. In this week's post, I thought I would list out the answers to some of the most frequently asked questions in this regard.

(1) Are View Legal deeds 'Bamford compliant' –every trust deed provided by View Legal is Bamford compliant.

(2) Are trust deeds from other providers Bamford compliant – this is an issue that will need to be assessed on a case by case basis. Certainly the older the deed, the less likely it is to be compliant. There are also a number of non tax specialist deed providers who have not traditionally focused on some of the critical issues raised in Bamford.

(3) Should we be looking to do wholesale updates of all trust deeds in our client base (similar to the recent super deed updates completed) –subject to the exact approach the ATO adopts in the decision impact statement that is due to be released shortly, we believe there is likely to be some benefit in at least conducting a full review of all deeds.

(4) Are there standard distribution minutes available – as many of you will be aware, we have always been conservative in our approach to distribution minutes and strongly recommend that every trustee should independently consider both the trust deed and the exact nature of distributions on a year on year basis (in other words, not use a 'standard' minute).

Certainly given the confirmation of the proportionate approach, the crafting of minutes so that (for example) infant beneficiaries get a set dollar amount and then the balance goes in certain percentages will rarely (if ever) be appropriate.

We are already working with a number of accounting practices to develop an approach that suits the risk profiles of their clients.

Trust distributions 101 – Read the deed!

Posted 10 May 2010

Last week, an accountant and I caught up in relation to his review of trust distributions in previous years for a new client to his firm.

The main issue related to income that had been passed to a company over a number of years.

While the trust deed allowed distributions to companies, it had a relatively unusual provision that required all of the shares in that company to be owned by the 'primary beneficiaries' set out in the schedule.

Unfortunately the company that had been used had a share structure that did not comply with the provisions of the deed and we were trying to explore if there were some potential solutions available.

Each idea we have come up with to date has not been particularly satisfactory, so this week's practical tip is simply to remember to ensure that whenever working with trust someone is responsible to 'read the deed'.

Unpaid present entitlements (UPE) and the election

Posted 16 August 2010

Last week, the National Institute of Accountants (**NIA**) sought to turn the UPE issue into an election topic.

An extract from the Weekly Tax Bulletin released on Friday is set out below.

It highlights, as many have, that the changed approach by the ATO effectively renders the specific provisions under Division 7A in relation to UPEs irrelevant.

> *The NIA has called on both political parties "to show their small business credentials and intervene to put a stop" to the ATO's changed view of the treatment of unpaid entitlements to corporate beneficiaries. The NIA said that Taxation Ruling TR 2010/3 now confirms the ATO view that unpaid present entitlements (UPE) to corporate beneficiaries will be treated as loans and potentially deeming them as unfranked dividends.*
>
> *NIA chief executive officer Andrew Conway said this new approach puts an end to a 12 year long standard practice of not treating unpaid entitlements to corporate*

beneficiaries as loans. "For the majority of cases the use of such funds by the trust is solely for business working capital related purposes. We have been reminded that the mischief which the ATO is trying to address is where these funds are used for private purposes within the trust," he said.

The NIA says there is strong evidence to indicate that it was never the intention of Div 7A to extend to UPEs and that "this latest change of heart by the ATO has no legislative basis". The ruling contradicts the underlying policy intent of Div 7A, the NIA said.

Streaming decision released

Posted 22 November 2010

There was confirmation last week from the Queensland Supreme Court that where a trust deed of a discretionary trust has appropriate powers and the trustee resolutions are appropriately crafted, a trustee can allocate franking credits differentially from net income.

For those interested the full title of the case is 'Thomas Nominees Pty Ltd ACN 010 049 788 v Thomas & Anor [2010] QSC 417' (Supreme Court of Qld, Applegarth J, 11 November 2010).

The decision turned to a large extent on the terms of the trust deed and the fact that the trustee:

a could treat franking credits as income of the trust capable of distribution;
b had discretion to distribute franking credits to different beneficiaries; and
c had the power to stream different categories of income between beneficiaries.

In light of the above powers, in brief terms, the key aspects of the decision were as follows:

(1) selective allocation of franking credits is possible under section 207-35 ITAA 1997;
(2) section 97 ITAA 1936 takes a proportionate approach to the distribution of net income (as set out in the Bamford decision);
(3) section 207-35 is an exception to Division 6 (and therefore section 97) ITAA 1936;
(4) franking credits need not follow the shares of net income included in a beneficiary's assessable income on an equal footing;

(5) net income (under section 95 ITAA 1936) does not need to exceed the franking credits included in assessable income for those credits to pass through to beneficiaries; and

(6) the ATO's comments that franking credits may not be able to form part of the income of a trust estate for trust law purposes because they are 'merely a tax concept which do not represent an accretion to the trust fund over and above the distributions to which they attach' could not be accepted;

(7) ultimately, franking credits were held to have some attributes of income under the tax legislation, therefore they could be dealt with by the trustee.

Bamford driven review of Tax Act

Posted 17 December 2010

While I had flagged there would be no further post this year, the Government has made a mid December announcement yesterday worth noting.

As you will read elsewhere, it has been confirmed that there will be a full review of the way in which trusts are taxed.

Relevant extracts of Bill Shorten's announcement are set out below.

While there is obviously a long way to go, it is reassuring that the rumoured revisiting of the entity taxation regime has been expressly ruled out.

(1) There are major uncertainties after Bamford, especially about the extent to which amounts derived by trustees retain their character (for example, as capital gains or franked dividends) when they flow through to beneficiaries.

(2) A public consultation process (has been announced) as the first step towards updating the trust income tax provisions in Division 6 of Part III of the Income Tax Assessment Act 1936 (ITAA 1936) and rewriting them into the 1997 Act.

(3) "In developing an initial consultation paper for release in the first part of 2011, Treasury will draw heavily on the expertise of the private sector, particularly through the established Tax Design Panel process and the Board of Taxation," said the Assistant Treasurer

(4) "The options to be canvassed in public consultation will be developed within the broad policy framework currently applying to the taxation of trust income".

(5) Any options will seek to ensure that net taxable income of a trust is assessed primarily to beneficiaries. Trustees will continue to be assessed only to the extent that amounts of net taxable income are not otherwise assessable to

beneficiaries. The options will not include the taxation of trusts as companies, which would be a major departure from the current law.

(6) "Based on advice I have sought from the Board of Taxation, I will also consider further whether there are any issues that must be addressed in this current tax year".

(7) "Trust tax law has been an ongoing issue for some time and it is important to simplify the system, rewrite the rules and give more certainty to the many thousands of small businesses and farmers who use trusts. I encourage all interested stakeholders to make a submission to the consultation".

UPE deadline day rapidly approaching

Posted 9 May 2011

Over the last couple of weeks, we have seen a significant increase in the level of enquiry about the appropriate strategies to adopt for clients that have trusts with unpaid present entitlements (UPE) owing to corporate beneficiaries.

For some months leading advisers have recommended that any specific steps be delayed for as long as possible on the basis (and hope) that there might be some relaxation or unwinding of the position adopted by the Tax Office. Indeed, there have also been rumours of a test case being run.

Given that it now appears increasingly likely that there will be nothing of substance changing the current rules before 30 June 2011, advisers and clients in this area now have less than eight weeks to have adopted one of the 'safe harbours' provided by the Tax Office.

ATO gives some relief in lead up to 30 June for trust distribution resolutions

Posted 29 June 2011

Extracted below is the announcement the ATO has made this morning confirming the transitional arrangements that will apply for 30 June 2011 in relation to trust distributions.

The comments in relation to IT 328 are particularly interesting.

Other administrative arrangements

The Commissioner recognises that the passage of this legislation so close to the end of the income year to which it will first apply gives trustees and practitioners little time to familiarise themselves with its content and to determine how it might affect the circumstances of a particular trust for that income year (that is, the 2010-11 income year).

Therefore, following representations from practitioners, and in recognition of the practical difficulties faced by them and by trustees as a result of the timing of the new law, the Commissioner will put in place the following administrative arrangements in respect of the application of the new law to the 2010-11 income year.

Specific entitlement to franked distributions

As regards the timing of recording such an entitlement for the 2010-11 income year, the Commissioner has agreed to adopt a similar approach to that set out in Income Tax Rulings IT 328 and 329 in respect of 'present entitlement' to trust income.

That is, for trusts with a 30 June balance date the Commissioner will accept that a relevant record made in respect of a franked distribution by 31 August 2011 meets the requirements of the new law for the 2010-11 income year in any case where ITs 328 and 329 would permit the trustee to take steps within that same period to make beneficiaries presently entitled to trust income for the purpose of Division 6.

For trusts that balance earlier than 30 June 2011 (or later than 30 June 2011 but before 31 August 2011) the Commissioner will likewise accept a relevant record made by 31 August 2011.

As the new law (if enacted as passed) will permit relevant records to be made in respect of capital gains no later than two months after the end of the relevant income year, there is no need for this arrangement to be extended to a beneficiary's specific entitlement to capital gains.

It should be noted that the arrangement outlined above concerning a beneficiary's specific entitlement to franked distributions will apply only for the 2010-11 income year.

Further, the Commissioner intends withdrawing ITs 328 and 329 for the 2011-12 and later income years.

Compliance action

Staff will also be instructed not to select cases for review or audit in respect of the 2010-11 income year for the sole purpose of determining whether the purported streaming of capital gains or franked distributions by a trustee is effective.

This instruction will not apply where there has been a deliberate attempt to exploit weaknesses or deficiencies in the law. In those cases we will apply the law as we understand it to operate.

We will also apply the law as we understand it to operate in any case that has been selected for review or audit for other reasons, and in preparing rulings or objections, and in arguing cases before the Tribunal or the courts.

Trust Distributions 101

Posted 20 March 2012

Last week's post touched on the Family Court decision from the end of 2011 concerning the way in which a family trust was treated as part of a matrimonial settlement.

One other aspect of the case that is worth mentioning involved the conclusion by the Court about the, purported, use of a corporate beneficiary.

In particular a 'bucket company' was set up some years after the initial establishment of the trust. The evidence that seemed to be accepted by the Court was that the company was established for 'tax minimisation or reduction purposes'.

Unfortunately, to the extent that a disgruntled third party (including the Tax Office) may wish to challenge the distributions, the company was not in fact a beneficiary of the trust.

While the 'wrongful' distributions (in the words of the Court) were not explored further in the context of this family law case, the comments highlight the theme of many earlier posts – that is in almost every area where structures are used (whether they be trusts, companies or super funds) it is critical that someone takes responsibility for reading the establishment documents before any step is taken.

Trust distributions and 30 June

Posted 8 July 2013

In the wash up of the passing of the financial year, an adviser contacted us last week with yet another reminder about the importance of reading trust deeds.

In this particular instance, the adviser had taken over a client from another firm. One of the key items on the trust checklist completed for every client of this adviser's firm is confirming what date the trust deed requires income distributions to have been made by.

The Tax Office has a long stated view that regardless of whatever concessions may be available under the tax legislation in terms of the due date for resolutions, these concessions are subject always to the trust instrument.

The terms of the trust deed here required all resolutions to be made by no later than 12pm on 29 June in the relevant financial year. Unfortunately, the distributions for each of the previous years had all been dated 30 June, which meant they were invalid under the deed.

The adviser was, therefore, required to begin the process for lodgement of amended returns, relying on the default provisions under the trust deed and sought our guidance on how to best address this.

Needless to say that the income determination for the current financial year was made and passed by resolution dated 28 June, so as to at least comply with the deed this year.

Trust distributions – 3 reminders for 30 June 2014

Posted 24 June 2014

For the fourth time in recent weeks we have been fortunate to have an article featured in the Weekly Tax Bulletin. This time it is by fellow View Legal Director Patrick Ellwood and I and is extracted below for those who do not otherwise have easy access.

As regularly addressed in the Weekly Tax Bulletin, a methodical approach is needed when preparing trust distribution resolutions to ensure the intended outcomes are achieved.

With another 30 June fast approaching, it is timely to consider 3 key issues often overlooked, namely:

(1) ensuring that the intended recipient of a distribution is in fact a valid beneficiary of the trust;
(2) avoiding distributions to beneficiaries who appear to be validly appointed under a trust deed, however are in a practical sense excluded; and
(3) complying with any timing requirements under a trust deed, regardless of what the position at law may otherwise be.

Further comments on each of these issues are set out in turn below.

Is the intended recipient a beneficiary?

A beneficiary is a person or entity who has an equitable interest in the trust fund. A beneficiary has enforceable rights against a trustee who fails to comply with their duties, regardless of whether they have ever received distributions of income or capital from the trust.

The range of eligible beneficiaries will generally be defined in the trust deed and the first step in any proposed distribution should be to ensure that the intended recipient falls within that defined range.

Once the range of eligible beneficiaries has been determined, the next step is to identify classes of specifically excluded beneficiaries.

These exclusions will usually override the provisions in a trust deed which create the class of potential beneficiaries and some common examples include:

(1) persons who have either renounced their beneficial interest or have been removed as a beneficiary of the trust fund;
(2) the settlor and other members of the settlor's family;
(3) any "notional settlor"; and
(4) the trustee.

A comprehensive review of a trust deed must include an analysis of every variation or resolution of a trustee or other person (such as an appointor) that may impact on the interpretation of the document.

The range of documents that could impact on the potential beneficiaries of a trust at any particular point in time is almost limitless. Some examples include:

(1) resolutions of the trustee to add or remove beneficiaries pursuant to a power in the trust deed;
(2) nominations or decisions of persons nominated in roles such as a principal, appointor or nominator; and
(3) consequential changes triggered by the way in which the trust deed is drafted (eg beneficiaries who are only potential beneficiaries while other named persons are living).

Does the intended recipient appear to be a beneficiary, yet practically is excluded?

It is important to remember that the unilateral actions of a potential beneficiary may impact on whether they can validly receive a distribution. For example, a named beneficiary may disclaim their entitlement to a distribution in any particular year, or may in fact renounce all interests under the trust.

There are also a number of potential issues that can arise in relation to beneficiaries that appear to have been nominated as beneficiaries, as to whether the nomination is effective. These issues can include:

(1) whether the appointment needs to be made in writing;
(2) whether the appointor has been validly appointed to their role;
(3) at what point the nomination needs to take place in the context of the timeframe within which a distribution must be made; and
(4) are there any consequential ramifications of the nomination, eg stamp duty, resettlement for tax purposes or asset protection.

Family trust election

In addition to the traditional trust law related restrictions on the potential beneficiaries of a trust, it is important to keep in mind the consequences of a trustee making a family trust election or interposed entity election.

Where such an election has been made, despite what might otherwise be provided for in the trust instrument, the election will effectively limit the range of potential beneficiaries who can receive a distribution without triggering a penal tax consequence (being the family trust distribution tax).

A family trust election will generally be made by a trustee for one or more of the following reasons:

a access to franking credits;
b ability to utilise prior year losses and bad debt deductions;
c simplifying the continuity of ownership test; and
d eliminating the need to comply with the trustee beneficiary reporting rules.

While a full analysis of the impact of family trust elections and interposed entity elections is outside the scope of this article, it is critical to consider the potential implications of any such election on what might otherwise appear to be a permissible distribution in accordance with the trust deed.

Complying with any timing requirements under the trust deed

Historically, the Commissioner permitted resolutions to be made after 30 June each year via longstanding ITs 328 and 329, however as practitioners will recall, these were withdrawn in 2011.

The current law does allow resolutions in relation to capital gains to be made no later than 2 months after the end of the relevant income year. Any other distributions, including in particular franked distributions, must be made by 30 June in the relevant income year.

Notwithstanding the general position above, the ATO has regularly confirmed its view that regardless of any timing concessions available under the tax legislation or ATO practice, these concessions are subject always to the provisions of the relevant trust instrument.

In recent times, we have reviewed a number of trust deeds by different providers that require all resolutions to be made by a date earlier than 30 June, e.g. no later than 12pm on 28 June in the relevant financial year. Unfortunately, in every situation we have seen, all distributions for previous income years were dated 30 June, meaning each resolution was in fact invalid under the deed, regardless of the fact that the resolution otherwise complied with the law.

In these situations, arguably the only practical solution is to proceed with lodgment of amended returns, relying on the default provisions under the trust deed – assuming there are adequate default provisions.

Some ramifications of failed trust distributions

Posted 21 October 2014

For those that do not otherwise have access to theWeekly Tax Bulletin, the most recent published article by fellowView LegalDirector Tara Lucke and I is extracted below.

As regularly addressed in the *Weekly Tax Bulletin*, a methodical approach is needed when preparing trust distribution resolutions to ensure the intended outcomes are achieved.

As explored at 2014 WTB 27 [942], there are a range of issues often overlooked in relation to distribution resolutions.

Where a purported trust distribution is subsequently found to be invalid, several potential ramifications arise, including:

- The "knowing recipient" principle.
- Disallowed deductions.
- Disclaimers.
- Equity and rectification.
- Impact of any default provisions.

Further comments on each of these issues are set out in turn below.

"Knowing recipient" principle

"Knowing recipient" is a principle that evolved out of situations where a trustee (who holds property on trust on behalf of the beneficiaries of a trust) appropriates trust funds for the benefit of a third party who has knowledge of the trust relationship.

The concept gives the "wronged" beneficiaries the right to make a personal claim against the third party on the basis that the third party received the trust property, whilst having knowledge of the relationship between the property in question, the trustee and the beneficiaries.

Impact of disallowed deductions

The treatment of disallowed deductions turns largely on the way in which the relevant distribution resolution is crafted.

Broadly, there are 3 possible outcomes, namely:

- the amounts representing the disallowed deductions will be validly distributed to a particular beneficiary via the provisions of a distribution resolution;

- the default provisions under the trust deed will regulate the distribution (further comments in this regard are set out below); or
- the amount will be treated as an accumulation to the trust and the trustee will be taxed at the highest marginal tax rate is applied.

Disclaimers

In *FCT v Ramsden* [2005] FCAFC 39, the court held that the purported disclaimers by particular beneficiaries were ineffective. However, it was confirmed that any interest acquired in the net income of a trust under the default provisions of a deed could be disclaimed by a beneficiary separately from any other entitlements which might accrue to that beneficiary under other provisions of the deed.

It was also confirmed that a disclaimer can be made retrospectively, provided it is made within a reasonable period of time from the beneficiary first becoming aware of the relevant interest that they wish to disclaim.

Equity and rectification

A court may use the equitable remedy of rectification where there is an error in a trust document which does not reflect the intentions of the parties and in turn, results in an invalid distribution.

In order for rectification to be granted, the party applying for the court to exercise its discretion must establish 3 elements:

- the intention that the parties had in relation to the document up until the time the distribution resolution was executed
- a mistake was made in the document that does not reflect the parties' true intentions; an
- if the rectification order was granted, it would correct the mistake and match the parties' intentions.

Importantly, rectification will not be granted where there is simply an inadvertent financial result that occurred due to a misunderstanding of the consequences of a deliberate act.

Default provisions

From a trust law perspective, default capital provisions, and in some cases, default income provisions, under discretionary trusts are generally seen as important to ensure that the trust is valid at law.

From a tax perspective, the main objective of a default distribution clause, particularly for income, is to ensure that the default beneficiaries are assessed on the failed distribution, rather than the trustee being assessed at the top marginal rate.

The case of *BRK (BRIS) PTY LTD v FCT* (2001) 46 ATR 347 is arguably the leading example in this regard. In this case, the default distribution clause of the relevant trust required, where there was a failure to distribute, that the trustee "divide the Fund equally among the beneficiaries named in the Schedule hereto".

However, the clause was crafted such that the distribution did not take place until a date after the end of a tax year.

Based on the drafting of the relevant clause, the court confirmed that while the provisions were valid from a trust law perspective, the trustee was unable to make the required distribution to the default beneficiaries until after the end of each tax year. This, in turn meant that all undistributed income was in fact effectively accumulated for tax purposes each tax year. Therefore, all undistributed income was taxed to the trustee at the top marginal rate.

Conclusion – start by reading the deed

Given the range of significantly adverse consequences that can result where a purported trust distribution is subsequently found to be invalid, advisers should proactively invest in processes and systems to minimise the risk of such an outcome.

Invariably, best practice dictates that in every situation before preparing a resolution there should be:

(1) a comprehensive review of the relevant trust deed including an analysis of every variation or resolution of a trustee or other person (such as a principal, appointor or guardian) that may impact on the interpretation of the trust document;

(2) specific review of the relevant tax legislation applicable to the amounts to be addressed by the resolution; and

(3) thought applied to the exact factual scenario that the trustee is addressing, in the context of the trust deed and tax laws.

Trust distributions – three reminders

Posted 12 May 2015

Previous posts have focused on the various key aspects in relation to trust distributions (see for example –

> *http://blog.viewlegal.com.au/2013/10/one-remedy-where-trust-distributions.html*
> *http://blog.viewlegal.com.au/2013/08/a-further-reminder-read-deed.html*
> *http://blog.viewlegal.com.au/2013/07/trust-distributions-and-30-june.html*)

As another 30 June looms, it is useful to note that one of the key aspects in this regard relates to the manner in which section 99 of the Tax Act causes the trustee of a discretionary trust to be taxed at the top marginal rate whenever an income year passes where no beneficiary is made presently entitled to the trust income for that year.

In this type of situation, it is critical to consider the way in which the relevant trust deed is crafted, and in particular:

(1) understanding if there is a default distribution provision in relation to income;
(2) if there is a default provision, ensuring that the potential default beneficiaries reflect the intentions of those ultimately in control of the trust;
(3) ensuring that the default provisions do in fact work.

Arguably, the leading case in this area is *BRK (Bris) Pty Ltd v FCT* [2001] FCA 164.

As usual, a full copy of the case is available at the following link ***http://www.austlii.edu.au/au/cases/cth/FCA/2001/164.html***.

While there was a purported default distribution, it was crafted to only apply if the trustee had not otherwise made a decision 'within a reasonable time after the end of a financial year'.

While the provision was likely valid for trust law purposes, it was ineffective for tax law purposes because section 99 imposes the top marginal tax rate for any undistributed income as at midnight on 30 June each financial year.

Trust distributions – is the recipient a beneficiary?

Posted 19 May 2015

Numerous previous posts have raised that the trustee of a discretionary trust must ensure that the intended recipient is in fact a potential beneficiary of the trust when making a trust distributive ***http://blog.viewlegal.com.au/2014/06/trust-distributions-3-reminders-for-30.html***

> ***http://blog.viewlegal.com.au/2013/09/read-deed-another-reminder-re-invalid.html***
> ***http://blog.viewlegal.com.au/2013/07/trust-distributions-and-30-june.html]***

As mentioned in last week's post, one of the most famous cases in this regard is *BRK (Bris) Pty Ltd v FCT* [2001] FCA 164.

In relation to the aspect of the decision in BRK that concerned the initial failure to make a valid distribution, the circumstances were as follows:

(1) The trustee had the power to make distributions amongst potential beneficiaries.
(2) The beneficiaries were listed in a schedule to the deed.
(3) The trustee believed it had the power to nominate additional beneficiaries, and indeed, prepared resolutions quoting particular clauses in the deed that gave it the requisite power.
(4) Unfortunately the trustee must have been referring to some other trust instrument, as the purported power to nominate additional beneficiaries did not in fact exist in the trust deed for the relevant trust.
(5) As the trustee did not have the relevant power to make the nomination resolution, the subsequent distribution resolution purporting to pass benefits to the invalidly nominated beneficiaries also failed.

Although it was unnecessary given the above conclusions, the court also noted that even if the trustee had the power that they purported to exercise in nominating the additional beneficiaries, the attempted resolution of income distribution would have failed in any event because:

a one of the beneficiaries nominated did not exist at the date of the distribution;
b the other beneficiary nominated was mis-defined (in particular, a company was noted as a trustee of a particular trust, however that company was not in fact acting as trustee for the trust at the date of nomination).

At last some clarity with the streaming of franking credits? But trust law re-write still urgently needed

Posted 8 September 2015

For those that do not otherwise have access to theWeekly Tax Bulletin, the further article from earlier this month by fellowView LegalDirector Patrick Ellwood and me is extracted below.

For ease of reference, an earlier post addressing a previous decision in this matter is at the following link –

http://blog.viewlegal.com.au/2010/11/streaming-decision-released.html

The recent case of *Thomas v FCT* [2015] FCA 968, reported in this *Bulletin*, considers a number of key issues relating to the distribution of franking credits by the trustee of a discretionary trust, including the ability to stream franking credits as a separate class of income.

It follows the well-publicised decision of the Queensland Supreme Court in *Thomas Nominees Pty Ltd ACN 010 049 788 v Thomas & Anor* [2010] QSC 417 (reported at 2010 WTB 49 [1884]), which relevantly held that franking credits could form part of the income of a trust estate for trust law purposes and be streamed to particular beneficiaries. The Commissioner was not a party to that earlier decision.

The *Thomas* case explores the interaction between s 95 and s 97 of the ITAA 1936 dealing with trust income and Div 207 of the ITAA 1997 dealing with the imputation system.

The decision is a timely reminder of the need to ensure that trust distributions are made in compliance with the trust deed, the ITAA 1936 and the ITAA 1997, and of the complexities that can arise when streaming different classes of income.

Facts

A more detailed summary of the facts of the case are set out separately in this *Bulletin*, however in brief, the trustee of Thomas Investment Trust purported to distribute the trust's income in several consecutive financial years as follows:

- Around 90% of the franking credits and foreign income and 1% of the remaining net income to an individual beneficiary.
- The balance of the net income to a corporate beneficiary.

The Commissioner challenged the effect of the distributions and in essence, argued that the franking credits could not be distributed to a beneficiary independently of the franked dividend to which those franking credits related.

The taxpayer contended that the franking credits were in fact a class of income capable of being streamed to particular beneficiaries in accordance with the trust instrument.

A number of other matters relating to the trust instrument and distribution resolutions were considered by the Court, which are beyond the scope of this article.

Outcome

The judgment, which the Commissioner at least is likely to believe is a thorough and well-crafted decision, rejects the earlier conclusion in *Thomas Nominees Pty Ltd ACN 010 049 788 v Thomas & Anor* [2010] QSC 417 and provides significant guidance in relation to the streaming of franked dividends and franking credits.

It is widely understood that Div 207-55(3) of the ITAA 1997 provides that a beneficiary's share of a franked distribution is equal to the amount included when determining the beneficiary's share of the trust's income under s 95 of the ITAA 1936.

Div 207 also recognises and permits a trustee to stream some or all of a franked dividend to one or more beneficiaries to the exclusion of others, subject to the requisite powers under the trust deed.

Provided the relevant trust instrument expressly permits streaming of franked dividends as a separate class of income, a trustee can choose to make one or more beneficiaries specifically entitled to franked dividends, while distributing other classes of income to different beneficiaries.

Any beneficiary who is made specifically entitled to franked dividends is then entitled to the benefit of the franking credits attaching to those dividends.

In *Thomas*, the trustee purported to stream franking credits as a separate class of income from the dividends themselves. This approach, permitted under the trust deed, saw one beneficiary receive the benefit of the tax offset under the imputation system at their marginal tax rate, while another beneficiary paid income tax on the dividend at the corporate tax rate.

The Court held that, although franking credits will generally have a clear commercial value to a beneficiary (as a result of the beneficiary's ability to claim a tax offset from the credit), a franking credit is not "income" for trust law purposes.

Specifically, although franking credits constitute statutory income for the purposes of the gross-up provisions, they are a notional, statutory creation in this regard and do not constitute "ordinary income" under trust law principles.

As a result, the operation of Div 207 makes it clear that franking credits can only "attach" to the franked dividend and cannot be streamed as a separate class of income, notwithstanding any other provision that may indicate to the contrary within the trust instrument.

The outcome of the case can perhaps be best summarised by the following quote from the judgment:

"What cannot occur if the tax offset is to be preserved...is an allocation of the s 95 net income amongst beneficiaries on a particular basis and a distribution of the franking credits otherwise attached or stapled to the franked dividends on **an entirely unrelated basis**, amongst the same beneficiaries." [Court's emphasis]

Lessons

A number of lessons can be taken from the case, including:

- As regularly highlighted in this *Bulletin*, ***it is critical to "read the deed"*** before purporting to exercise trust powers, particularly in relation to trust distributions.
- While reading the trust deed (including all valid variations) is necessary, it will ***not be sufficient by itself***. There are a myriad of related issues that need to be considered that may impact on the intended distribution, aside from whatever powers are set out in the trust instrument. Examples include renunciations and disclaimers by beneficiaries, purported changes that are not permitted under the relevant trust instrument (see for example the article at 2015 WTB 37 [1373] in relation to amending trust deeds) and the effective narrowing (for tax purposes) of permissible beneficiaries due to the impact of family trust and interposed entity elections.
- ***The wording of the distribution minute or resolution*** will be critical for determining the consequences of the distribution. Terms like "income" and "net income" will be defined differently depending on the trust instrument (even deeds that have been sourced from the same provider) and failing to understand those distinctions can result in inadvertent adverse outcomes for the trustee and beneficiaries.
- Distribution resolutions must also be crafted ***with reference to the trust instrument***, trust law principles, the ITAA 1936 and the ITAA 1997. For example, with increasing regularity, we are seeing trust deeds that require distributions take place *before* they are otherwise needed under the ITAA.
- Trustees should act with significant care when dealing with ***"notional" amounts*** such as franking credits, to ensure the intended tax and commercial objectives are achieved.
- Trustees have a duty to ensure they are aware of their ***rights and responsibilities*** under the trust deed and the limitations under the ITAA 1936 and the ITAA 1997. A failure to discharge this duty can mean a trustee is personally liable.
- Ultimately however the latest instalment in this series of cases (so far) also highlights the need for the Government to prioritise the long awaited rewrite of the legislation governing the taxation of trusts in order to simplify what continues to be an unnecessarily complex area of the taxation law.

Chapter 3(c)

TRUSTS – INTERPRETATION

Trust deed tip

Posted 3 June 2010

Again this last week, we have had some more issues arise in relation to family trusts.

As is often the case, the issue from this week was identified by a financier.

The issue arose due to a review of some historical variation deeds to the original trust documents.

Due to a relatively unusual provision, the original trust required that any variation could only be made with the consent of the settlor (i.e. the person who originally set up the trust) and all of the 'primary' beneficiaries who were set out in the schedule to the trust.

None of the earlier variations had received consent from any of the relevant parties.

The solution (which is still to be approved by the bank) was to implement a comprehensive deed of confirmation and obtain signatures from all relevant people – fortunately, the settlor was still alive and willing to assist.

Next week, I will touch on some other practical difficulties that we are going to need to consider and possibly address in the future.

Further trust deed tips

Posted 21 June 2010

Last week, I mentioned the trust where a number of variations had been implemented over the years, but those variations did not comply with the rules set out under the trust instrument.

The short term fix (in order to satisfy financier requirements) was to implement a deed of confirmation of the historical changes.

To try and minimise future difficulties, we are also implementing the following:

(1) With the settlor's consent (given that he is still alive and has capacity to do so), we are removing the requirement for him to consent to any future changes. This step has some potential tax and stamp duty consequences, however on balance, the client's accountant has agreed with us that it is the most logical next step.

(2) We are also clarifying the requirements around the consent of primary beneficiaries. For this particular situation, all primary beneficiaries are currently over the age of 18 and alive, however the client did not want a situation in the future where there were infant beneficiaries (or

beneficiaries that no longer were alive) given third parties might seek to challenge whether a future purported variation was in fact effective without the consent of those people.

Trust deed updates – Start at the start

Posted 17 September 2010

Due to the recent decision in Bamford, we have seen a significant increase in the number of advisers recommending to their clients that a complete review of, particularly family trusts, be done for each client.

As part of this review process, there is often a subsequent recommendation that the trust deed needs to be updated for all recent changes in the law, or at the least to make the deed 'Bamford compliant'.

Previous posts have touched on some of the issues that arise in this regard. Last week, I was reminded, however, about the importance of getting the basics right in relation to any deed update.

Arguably the most fundamental issue that needs to be considered in any deed update is whether there is in fact a power to vary the document.

There are an amazing number of trust deeds that, for whatever reason, in fact do not have any power to vary under them at all.

In these situations, the only way to amend the trust deed is to apply to court – which is obviously an expensive and time consuming exercise. In some situations however, it is a step that commercially must in fact be taken.

Next week, I will detail two further issues that arise in relation to deed updates that should also be kept in mind.

When a power to vary is not a power to vary

Posted 24 September 2010

Last week, we touched on the fact that many trust deeds do not have any power to vary in them.

There are similarly many trusts that do have a power to vary, but that power to vary is not as comprehensive as may otherwise be assumed.

Two recent examples that we have seen are summarised below.

The first example (which was highlighted in quite a high profile case last year) turns on whether a power to vary extends to all aspects of the trust instrument. In particular, some powers to vary are restricted to either:

(1) The formal provisions that actually establish the terms of the trust.
(2) Alternatively, the power to vary might be restricted to the actual powers that the trustee has to run the trust.

Care should always therefore be taken to understand exactly how comprehensive the power to vary is.

Similarly, some powers to vary are subject to specific prohibitions. For example, a power might extend to all parts of a trust other than the rules regulating the appointor provision.

In these types of situations, it is generally impossible (unless court approval is obtained to vary the relevant clause), even if the affected party (for example the appointor) were to consent to the variation.

Ultimately (and generally in complete contrast to superannuation trust deed variations), there is always the need to very carefully review the exact basis on which any purported variation to a family trust is to be implemented before making a change.

Small i income

Posted 18 July 2011

A number of posts over the last 18 months have touched on various aspects of the Bamford decision.

One issue that comes up more frequently than otherwise might be assumed is the way in which the word 'income' is used throughout a trust deed.

Somewhat concerningly, we have seen a number of instances where, although there is a definition of 'income', the word defined is mentioned in a capitalised sense – in other words, where the intention under the deed exists, then the word income will start with a capital I.

When reference is then had however to the distribution of income provisions, the deed drafter has not in fact used the 'big I' income definition, but rather has simply referred to 'small i' income.

Obviously, there are a number of potentially complex trust law interpretation issues that can arise in this regard. Our initial view in many of these situations however is that it is arguably going to be quite clear what position the Tax Office will take.

ATO reminder – read the deed

Posted 9 July 2012

Following on from the recent posts about the ATO draft determination on resettlements (TD2012/D4), today's post is in effect a further reminder of an earlier post that focused on the catch phrase 'Read the Deed', again with thanks to co View Legal director Tara Lucke.

One of the key themes in the recent ATO determination is that a trust variation must be made within the scope of the variation power in the trust deed.

If a purported variation is made outside the scope of the particular variation power, the ATO has provided guidance that this may result in the termination of a trust (i.e. a resettlement for CGT purposes).

We are constantly encountering deeds that have significant limitations on the variation power, particularly with the regular amendments we are doing for clients of accounting firms to ensure that trust deeds are up-to-date for all recent changes in law.

Next week's post will focus on some of the common variation prohibitions we come across.

Prohibitions on trust deed variations

Posted 16 July 2012

As mentioned last week, we often find trust deeds have prohibitions on a trustee's ability to vary the document.

Some of the issues to be aware of in this regard include:

(1) Often variations can only be made with the consent of someone other than the trustee, for example an appointor, guardian or even the settlor.
(2) In some cases, variations can only be made to the core (or trust) provisions of the deed, as opposed to the more general powers, which will usually limit the ability to vary the income provisions.
(3) Alternatively, while powers can be added to a trust, a deed will sometimes provide that any existing powers cannot be varied – this can be particularly problematic where there is a desire to update the income distribution provisions.

(4) There are countless other examples of restrictions on variations and indeed, we have come across deeds where there is a blanket prohibition on making variations to the deed, or at least on variations to particular clauses in the deed.

While there are often workarounds no matter what restriction is imposed, the fundamental rule to remember is that each and every deed must be read before embarking on a variation.

Appointor succession – choose wisely

Posted 4 March 2013

With thanks to co View Legal director Tara Lucke, today's post looks at how the role of the appointor is often the most important to consider when establishing or reviewing a trust. There does not necessarily need to be an appointor provision under a trust deed, however where there is, a trust deed will normally set out in some detail the way in which the role of appointor is dealt with on the death or incapacity of the person (or people) originally appointed.

Failing to understand succession arrangements of an appointor can create a range of difficulties as highlighted in the recent case of Montevento Holdings Pty Ltd v Scaffidi (2012) HCA 48. A full copy of the case is available at ***http://www.austlii.edu.au/au/cases/cth/HCA/2012/48.html***

The case concerned a challenge by a beneficiary of a discretionary trust to a change of trustee by the appointor. The challenging beneficiary was Guiseppe Scaffidi who, along with Maria (his mother) and Eugenio (his brother), was within the range of potential beneficiaries of the Scaffidi Family Trust.

The original appointor of the trust was Antonio Scaffidi (the father). On Antonio's death, Maria became the appointor and by deed Maria subsequently appointed Eugenio Scaffidi as the appointor.

After his appointment, Eugenio appointed Montevento Holdings Pty Ltd (a company of which he was the sole director and shareholder) as the sole trustee, effectively giving him complete control over the trust and its assets.

Guiseppe's challenge to the appointment of the trustee company ultimately failed before the High Court, essentially because the appointment complied with the provisions of the trust deed. The decision highlights that the role of appointor can often give ultimate control of a trust. Furthermore, it is a timely reminder of the importance of regularly reviewing the appropriateness of the appointor role in the context of succession planning, particularly where multiple beneficiaries are arguably intended to benefit from a discretionary trust over time.

The mechanics of the decision will be explored further in next week's post.

Appointor succession – read the deed

Posted 11 March 2013

As highlighted in previous posts, it is critical to 'read the deed' when providing advice that involves a trust.

Following last week's post (and again with thanks to Tara Lucke) about Montevento Holdings, this post reinforces the importance of reading a trust deed before taking any step.

In Montevento Holdings, a disgruntled beneficiary sought to rely on a technical interpretation of the way the appointor could exercise their power under the trust deed to change the trustee to support the argument that the change was ineffective.

The relevant clause precluded individual appointors from personally being appointed as trustee. As mentioned last week, the individual appointor appointed a company as trustee of which he was personally the sole director and shareholder.

The High Court held that the ordinary and natural meaning of the clause was that an individual person holding the office of appointor could not personally appoint themselves as trustee. However, because the trust deed consistently distinguished between individuals and companies, it did not prohibit the appointment of a corporate trustee, even if that trustee was controlled by the individual appointor.

A further reminder – read the deed

Posted 5 August 2013

As regular readers are aware, there have been numerous posts highlighting the importance of reading trust deeds and recently we had (yet another) reminder.

Many advisers would be aware that, particularly for deeds established in New South Wales (due to the stamp duty rules there), there is often a prohibition on any trustee, and in some instances any former trustee, being a beneficiary of a trust.

The example that came up again recently (it seems to be one that comes up every few weeks) involved an individual trustee of a standard family discretionary trust.

That individual trustee was also the sole primary beneficiary and sole appointor.

While there were potential issues from an asset protection perspective that we were reviewing, the more fundamental concern was that under the trust deed the trustee was specifically prohibited from ever receiving any income or capital distributions. A brief review of the balance sheet of the trust showed that substantial distributions had in fact been made to the trustee as primary beneficiary over a number of years.

There are now a myriad of issues that the trustee and his adviser are needing to work through, not least of which being how to address the enquiries of the lawyers for the trustee's former spouse who are alleging a breach of trust and what steps will need to be taken from a tax perspective in relation to the various years in which invalid distributions have taken place.

Read the deed – another reminder re invalid distributions

Posted 10 September 2013

For those that do not otherwise have access to the Weekly Tax Bulletin, the article from last week extracted below.

Practitioners will be aware, from many previous articles in this Bulletin (and elsewhere), of the critical importance that trust deeds should be read before making any distribution of income or capital. While the "read the deed" mantra should be indelibly etched in practitioners' minds, regular reminders of the dangers of not doing this are not out of place.

One example of a family law case of Harris v Harris [2011] FamCAFC 245 where the range of potential beneficiaries was critical was profiled in our article at 2012 WTB 39 [1586].

In that case, the trial judge in a family court matter noted that the recipient of trust distributions (being a company), who was being challenged, was not in fact an eligible beneficiary of the relevant trust. If the company had been simply nominated as a potential beneficiary, then the distributions would have most likely been valid.

A more common example of where difficulties with invalid distributions arise, however, relates to where particular potential beneficiaries are in fact expressly excluded by the trust deed. The most common example in this regard is the exclusion of the trustee, be that the current, former or even a future trustee, from being a beneficiary of a trust.

These types of clauses are often found in deeds prepared by New South Wales advisers. This is primarily because s 54(3) of the Duties Act 1997 (NSW) limits the nominal duty exemption for a change of trustee to trust deeds that contain provisions ensuring that:

(1) none of the continuing trustees remaining after the appointment of a new trustee are or can become a beneficiary under the trust;
(2) none of the trustees of the trust after the appointment of a new trustee are or can become a beneficiary under the trust; and
(3) the transfer is not part of a scheme for conferring an interest, in relation to the trust property, on a new trustee or any other person, whether as a beneficiary or otherwise, to the detriment of the beneficial interest or potential beneficial interest of any person.

An example of a clause adopting an approach that ensures access to the stamp duty relief is as follows:

"The Trustee for the time being of the Trust can not be a beneficiary of the Trust. None of the continuing Trustees remaining after the retirement of a Trustee is or can become a beneficiary under the Trust, and none of the Trustees of the Trust after the appointment of a new Trustee is or can become a beneficiary under the Trust."

New South Wales is the only Australian jurisdiction that has this type of restriction on accessing the duty concessions for a change of trustee and, understandably, clauses drafted in this manner are extremely prevalent with deed providers or lawyers based in New South Wales.

In many instances, however, there may in fact be no other connection with New South Wales for anyone associated with the trust.

The risks created by this drafting approach will, therefore, often be less than obvious.

Anecdotally, there would seem to be an increasing number of situations where invalid distributions are being discovered that stretch back over many years and involve significant levels of invalid distributions.

The exact ramifications of this type of situation will depend on a range of issues, including how any default provision under the relevant trust deed is crafted. This said, an embracing by all advisers involved with the administration of the trust of the mantra "read the deed" would avoid the issue ever arising in the first place.

Always 'read the deed'

Posted 15 September 2015

The recent decision of *Mercanti v. Mercanti* [2015] WASC 297 again reinforces the mantra 'read the deed', which is a theme that has featured regularly in previous posts (see for example – ***http://blog.viewlegal.com.au/2014/03/death-benefit-nominations-read-deed.html***, ***http://blog.viewlegal.com.au/2013/08/a-further-reminder-read-deed.html***, ***http://blog.viewlegal.com.au/2012/07/ato-reminder-read-deed.html***).

As usual, a full copy of the decision is available via the following link – ***http://www.austlii.edu.au/au/cases/wa/WASC/2015/297.html***

Broadly the background was as follows –

(1) As part of a family succession plan, two family discretionary trusts were amended by deleting the original definition of 'appointor' for each trust.
(2) This resulted in the father being replaced by his son as appointor of the two trusts.
(3) The appointor power under each trust gave the person nominated the power to unilaterally change the trustee of each trust.
(4) A later family dispute saw the son purport to exercise the appointor powers under each trust deed (as amended) to replace the trustees with a company he controlled.
(5) The father attempted to resist the changes, in part on the basis that the earlier deeds of variation were not in accordance with the variation power in the trust deeds and therefore invalid.

In deciding that the change of appointor was valid under one trust deed, and invalid under the other, the court highlighted the overriding importance of reading the relevant trust instrument. In particular –

a One deed had a variation power that relevantly provided the ability to 'vary all or any of the trusts, terms and conditions'. The scope of this provision was sufficiently wide to allow the original change of appointor and therefore the son was able to use his power to change the trustee.
b The power under the second deed however only provided the ability to 'vary all or any of the trusts'. In other words, there was no express power to amend the terms and conditions of the trust deed.
c The concept of 'trusts' does not ordinarily, and did not here, extend to the appointor clauses, meaning the purported variation of appointor was invalid and in turn the son's attempted change of trusteeship ineffective.

In many respects the decision here is simply the application of principles explained in detail in the case of *Jenkins v Ellett* [2007] QSC 154, which will be the subject of next week's post.

Another reminder to 'read the deed'

Posted 22 September 2015

As highlighted in last week's post, the need to 'read the deed' before making any variation to a trust deed is critical (see – ***http://blog.viewlegal.com.au/2015/09/always-read-deed.html***).

The case (*Jenkins v Ellett* [2007] QSC 154) mentioned in passing, in a previous post (see – ***http://blog.viewlegal.com.au/2010/09/when-power-to-vary-is-not-power-to-vary.html***) and again last week, remains a leading example of this mantra.

As usual, a full copy of the decision is available via the following link –

http://www.austlii.edu.au/au/cases/qld/QSC/2007/154.html

Broadly the situation in this case was as follows:

A principal under a trust deed had the ability to remove and appoint the trustee of the trust.

The principal purported to rely on a power of variation to remove himself as principal and name a replacement, which effectively changed the schedule to the trust deed that automatically appointed the principal's legal personal representative (**LPR**) as his replacement on death.

When the LPR of the principal purported to exercise the principal powers following the death of the original principal and was challenged, the Court held that the previous attempted variation was invalid, effectively confirming the LPR's authority to act as the principal.

The attempted variation was held to be invalid because the relevant power in the trust deed was crafted so that it could only be used in relation to the 'trusts declared', and in particular did not extend to varying the schedule to the trust deed.

Chapter 3(d)

TRUSTS – GENERAL

Typos and big legal bills

Posted 23 April 2010

Last Friday ended up being a very long day and unnecessarily expensive (both in terms of time consumed and bank, accounting and legal charges).

The day was also a particularly frustrating one due to the relatively underwhelming cause of all the hassle – a typo in an on-line created trust deed.

While the typo was not ours, it served as an extremely timely reminder of how critical it is to get even the simple things right.

One examples often mentioned in this space (based on a real life situation) where the vesting (or ending) date of a trust was accidentally noted as **18** years instead of the more standard **80** years.

Last Friday, the error (which had been generated by a client's former accountant using an online trust provider) was simply the spelling of the name Stephen with a 'v' instead of the 'ph' in the schedule.

While the trust had borrowed money from the bank before, no one had ever picked up on this typo.

Friday was the settlement day for a relatively large transaction and mid morning a Sydney bank officer identified the typo and insisted that the bank security could not be perfected because of it until the error was remedied.

After much (often quite illogical) negotiation, the bank finally agreed to a deed of variation being implemented.

As is often the way in these situations however, the deed (which ran to less than two sentences of actual substantive terms) was redrafted three times to satisfy the precise requirements of the bank.

Furthermore, even having produced the deed, there was the threat of the bank refusing to settle unless it was stamped prior to settlement.

The irony here of course is that the particular form of document is not liable to stamp duty in Queensland and due to recent changes at the Stamps Office trying to discourage people to lodge these documents for duty assessment (I might touch on this in more detail next week), it was going to be impossible to achieve a same day stamping.

Finally, based on a written undertaking provided by us, the bank did agree to settle.

Deeds of variation and stamp duty

Posted 4 May 2010

As I flagged last week, we had a very difficult Friday before last – all triggered by a very simple typo in the schedule to a trust deed.

One aspect that proved unnecessarily difficult due to the particular approach of the relevant bank officer was in relation to stamping.

Most Australian states (and particularly Queensland where this transaction was taking place) do not require administrative type changes to trusts to be charged with stamp duty.

In fact, in Queensland, recent changes have been made by the Stamps Office to actively discourage people from lodging these types of documents for assessment, given that the assessment is going to be returned as no duty payable.

Essentially then the only types of trust variations that need to be lodged for assessment in Queensland are ones that historically have been loosely described as 'resettlements'.

Practically, there is in fact no definition of a resettlement under the stamp duty rules and instead there is a series of other, relatively technical, provisions that need to be considered. For those interested in the general way in which these rules operate, please let me know and I can direct you to the relevant parts of the Stamps Office website.

When is a trust not a trust

Posted 5 October 2010

One adviser contacted me after the post last week about powers of variation and sent a trust deed for a brief initial review to our office.

For probably the 5th or 6th time in recent years, we discovered a situation where the trust itself had in fact already ended.

In other words, the vesting day for the trust had passed and, unfortunately, neither the client nor the adviser had realised that this event had taken place.

Practically the easy answer to whether the power to vary was wide enough, was easy to answer – in particular, it was irrelevant as there was in fact no longer a trust.

The more problematic issues however revolved around how exactly the income and capital of the trust should have been dealt with over the last 3 years since the trust had ended and what the trust law issues, liability issues, tax issues and stamp duty issues were likely to be.

Review of trustee's decision

Posted 8 August 2011

Last week, we had to assist a trustee of a family trust in their attempt to resist a review of a decision by a disgruntled beneficiary.

Many will be aware of the High Court decision in *Finch v Telstra Super Pty Ltd* [2010] HCA 36 –link to the case is as follows:

http://www.austlii.edu.au/au/cases/cth/HCA/2010/36.html

In very broad terms, we confirmed to the trustee the relatively settled position that seems to have evolved in this area, namely that the exercise of a discretion by a trustee is not subject to review by the courts unless one of the following three factors is present:

(1) The trustee does not act in good faith;
(2) The trustee does not give real and genuine consideration to the exercise of the discretion and the purposes for which the discretion was granted; or
(3) Reasons for the decision are provided by the trustee, but those reasons are unsound.

Trust establishment 101

Posted 30 March 2012

With thanks to co View Legal director Patrick Ellwood, this week's post concerns a recent land tax case (*Aston (Aust) Properties Pty Ltd v Commissioner of State Revenue*, for a full copy of the judgment follow this link – ***http://www.austlii.edu.au/au/cases/vic/VCAT/2012/48.html***) that highlights how critical it is to ensure that new structures are established correctly.

In this particular instance the taxpayer was arguing that group land tax assessments were incorrect due to the ownership of various landholdings being via separate trusts.

The trusts that were alleged to exist were prepared by the taxpayer himself and he gave evidence that he had 'become convinced that the process of creating multi tiered trust structures could be undertaken in an efficient manner without the need to purchase off the shelf trust deeds from solicitors'.

For a myriad of reasons the court held that the grouped land tax assessment was valid and that the purported trusts simply did not exist.

Some of the reasons the court concluded no trusts existed included:

(1) there was no evidence of any settlement sum being contributed on the initial creation of the trusts;
(2) no evidence could be shown in relation to funds changing hands or creation of bank accounts;
(3) while the trusts were purported to be created via schedules that were recreated on numerous occasions with reference to 'standard terms', the link to the standard terms could not be shown;
(4) of the documents that could be produced, there were a significant number of errors and inconsistencies; and
(5) some transactions that had purportedly been entered into were by entities that did not exist.

With the aid of hindsight each of these difficulties identified by the court could have been very easily addressed by getting some level of specialist advice prior to the creation of the trusts.

Settlement sums

Posted 17 April 2012

Last week, following on from the post before Easter, we had a enquiry about the consequences of a failure to deposit the settlement sum on the establishment of a discretionary trust.

This area of the law is potentially complex, however ultimately the conservative position is that the settlement sum should always be deposited into the trust's bank account, and ideally, it should in fact be the first deposit.

The approach of placing the settlement cheque (or a cash equivalent of it) on the file for the trust can be problematic for a range of reasons, including:

(1) Where the settlement sum is by way of cheque, the cheque will normally go stale after 13 months; and
(2) Even where cash is stored with the trust, it is difficult to provide documentary evidence of the settlement sum forming part of the trust if the cash is lost.

Ensuring that the settlement sum is deposited into the bank account of the trust at least avoids each of these two issues.

Void trusts

Posted 28 May 2012

Following on from recent posts, a further issue has come up over the last few days which relates to where a discretionary trust does not have any default provisions that apply for the distribution of capital.

The issues in this regard are quite complex, however like earlier posts, the conservative position is clear – i.e. every discretionary trust should ideally have clear provisions that apply for the distribution of capital in the event that a trustee fails to make a valid distribution.

The position in relation to default provisions for income is not as clear – often where there are no fallback provisions for income, an undistributed amount will simply form part of the capital of the trust.

This said, particularly following the High Court's decision in Bamford, we have seen a number of advisers focus very carefully on all of the core provisions of their client's trust deeds and the complete absence of a default distribution of capital, or in some instances, a purported default distribution that does not operate effectively, can be a trigger for looking to at least minimise the assets that are acquired in a trust moving forward.

Discretionary trust deeds health check

Posted 18 June 2012

Over time, View Legal has developed a 'trust review checklist' that outlines some of the key issues which should be considered as part of a general 'health check' of a discretionary trust deed to ensure it aligns with the constantly evolving legal requirements regarding trusts and tax implications.

An adviser after reading the document made contact in relation to the potential outcomes in the event a trustee fails to make a resolution.

We confirmed that there are the two main potential outcomes; namely that the trustee is taxed or the default beneficiaries are taxed. Which of the two outcomes applies will depend on how the trust deed is crafted.

In this regard, the leading case in this area is Ramsden.

The deed in Ramsden provided that a purported default distribution did not actually operate on its face and therefore the trustee was taxed at the top marginal rate. This can be a particularly poor outcome where there are capital gains given there is no entitlement to the 50% discount.

Conversely, we have seen many situations where the default provisions apply such that all distributions are made to a corporate beneficiary.

To the extent that there are capital gains that would otherwise be entitled to the 50% discount, this outcome will trigger adverse (and unnecessary) tax costs.

One other issue to be aware of, which again reinforces the importance of reading a deed, is that the actual timing of the resolution must be in accordance with the deed, even if legislation or Tax Office practice otherwise permits a later date.

For those interested to review the abovementioned summary go to the 'learn' and then 'resources' tabs of the View Legal website (www.viewlegal.com.au)

The next post will look at the Tax Office Determination released last week on trust variations.

What are the options in relation to deed updates post Bamford

Posted 15 October 2012

One issue that is raised regularly is the updating family trusts after the Bamford decision and related legislation.

The post today is the first in a series of 4 posts via the following video link under the heading 'What are the options in relation to deed updates post Bamford'. If you would like a link to the video please let me know.

As with other video posts, for those that do not have easy access to the streaming or would otherwise prefer to read the transcript, this is set out below –

What it actually means in terms of the trust variations, we think it's one of the following three things.

The first one, we're probably guess that most of the people we work with adopt this path, is to 'do nothing at all'.

Is that still the right thing to do? The honest answer is we don't know.

What we do know is even within the last 6 weeks, this complete review of trusts, that has been threatened forever, has already been pushed out for another year. So the earliest that we're going to have a new taxation regime for trusts is 2014.

You wouldn't want to take too heavy a bet for whether that's going to be pushed back again. I suspect there's every chance you're going to have an election before the next time around and you may well have a change of government.

So there's a whole range of things that are going to potentially happen between now and 2014 that will push that out.

The first one is to just do nothing.

The next post will look at this approach in more detail.

The "do nothing" approach to deed updates

Posted 22 October 2012

The post today is the 2nd in a series of 4 posts via the following video link under the heading 'The "do nothing" approach to deed updates'. If you would like a link to the video please let me know.

As with other video posts, for those that do not have easy access to the streaming or would otherwise prefer to read the transcript, this is set out below –

There are obvious advantages to 'doing nothing'.

From a cost perspective for a client, you would intuitively think that's probably the best outcome for them. Our only asterisk that we would put next to that is it does put enormous amount of pressure back on your practice and your team if someone needs to be sitting down and reading the deed.

Even if you've had the same provider for many years, you can almost guarantee that they will have changed their document, and they won't necessarily be able to tell you at what point at time they changed it.

Even if they could tell you, it probably doesn't absolve you under your insurance policy to say that everyone before a point in time will have this style of deed. Someone has to sit down and look at that. Which then means, according to the Tax Office, you can't just be churning out standard resolutions. You've actually got to have a tailored resolution that fits the particular deed and the particular income profile for the particular year.

So yes, the do nothing is attractive on a number of levels, but you need to be aware that it does add compliance costs.

You will see there's a common theme to all of these 3 choices.

Ultimately, our positioning is 'don't shoot the messenger'. This is something that has been imposed on us from Canberra. It means the cost of running a trust is more. So first one is to do nothing.

The next post will look at the second main approach we are seeing in this area.

Deed updates by exception post Bamford

Posted 29 October 2012

The post today is the 3rd instalment of 4 in this series of posts via the following video link under the heading 'Deed updates by exception post Bamford'. If you would like a link to the video please let me know.

As with other video posts, for those that do not have easy access to the streaming or would otherwise prefer to read the transcript, this is set out below –

The second approach is 'by exception', that is you do something. So on the basis that even if you do nothing, you've got to do something; which is you've got to have someone read the deed.

The by exception approach is if it's a particularly nasty deed, or there is as particularly big capital gain this year we're going to invest in this and we're going to look at it and we're possibly going to amend it, because of the particular circumstances.

We're going to do that, because even doing nothing, we've actually sat down and looked at the document and we understand it.

The trigger for a lot of people on that, if you're looking for a date, but don't quote me because again not all deed providers were diligent in doing this, but by and large, any deed after 1993, from any even remotely reputable provider, will have streaming.

So if you're looking for a date to say I would hope to be basically right, you can use 1993 as the date, because that's when streaming ruling came out or whatever it was and most deed providers across the board went through and did it. Indeed, a lot of them went and did actual updates in 1993. So even your pre-'85 trusts had gone and had that amendment in 1993.

The next post will look at the third main approach we are seeing in this area.

Wholesale deed updates post Bamford

Posted 05 November 2012

The post today is the 4th and final one in this series of posts via the following video link under the heading 'Wholesale deed updates post Bamford'. If you would like a link to the video please let me know.

As with other video posts, for those that do not have easy access to the streaming or would otherwise prefer to read the transcript, this is set out below –

The third idea is the 'wholesale update' approach.

The providers around are saying for $x you can go and get all of your deeds across the board 2012 compliant, really adopting the same approach that you do with an SMSF trust deed. People accept that with an SMSF, you're going to have to update it every 5 years probably. That's just the life that you lead running an SMSF.

We would argue that people have never really had that attitude with family trusts. Whether that's right or wrong is another question. But by and large, people have not really had that wholesale approach. We'll speak about Clark and why that may be the case from a resettlement perspective.

What we're saying with the third option is that you just go and do the update for all clients. Are you running the risk that you'll have to go and do that again in 3 or 4 years' time? Absolutely you are. But in the meantime, are you investing in your clients by saying you will read the deed once, make sure that every deed across the entire client base has the exact same provisions, can start getting some efficiencies in terms of resolutions, in terms of the review process.

It may be a little bit of pain upfront, however hopefully, any subsequent changes won't be too prohibitive anyway and many are saying may be this is the way to go.

Extensions to vesting dates – some lessons from Re Arthur Brady Family Trust; Re Trekmore Trading Trust

Posted 11 November 2014

For those that do not otherwise have access to the Weekly Tax Bulletin, the most recently published article by fellow View Legal Director Patrick Ellwood and I is extracted below.

Often a key reason for seeking to extend the vesting day of a trust will be to defer the likely tax and stamp duty implications that would arise where the trust vests and assets are distributed to the beneficiaries.

The recent Queensland case of *Re Arthur Brady Family Trust; Re Trekmore Trading Trust* [2014] QSC 244 (see 2014 WTB 42 [1416]), provides a useful illustration of the way in which the Courts respond to applications where deferring revenue costs are arguably the primary driver for the application.

The case follows previous decisions such as *Stein v Sybmore Holdings Pty Ltd* [2006] NSWSC 1004 in NSW and *Re Plator Nominees Pty Ltd* [2012] VSC 284 in Victoria, each of which are discussed below.

Legislation

In each State, the Court has statutory power to vary trust instruments in particular circumstances.

In the Northern Territory, this power can be exercised where the Court "thinks fit".

In Western Australia and Queensland, the power can be exercised where the Court considers the variation "expedient" or where the transaction is in "the best interests of the beneficiaries".

In all other jurisdictions, the "expedient" test applies.

In circumstances where a trust has been established with a vesting period of less than 80 years, the trustee may vary the trust deed, in accordance with an express power of variation in the trust instrument, to extend the vesting day.

The decision of FCT v Clark [2011] FCAFC 5 provides comfort that in many circumstances, such a variation will not trigger a resettlement of the trust for tax purposes.

However where the trust instrument does not provide the trustee with adequate powers to extend the vesting day, an application to the Court may be necessary.

The Court would therefore need to consider whether the trustee's reasons for wanting to extend the vesting day are "expedient" or "in the best interests of the beneficiaries", depending on the jurisdiction.

Cases

Stein v Sybmore Holdings Pty Ltd *involved an application under s 81 of the* Trustee Act 1925 *(NSW) to extend the vesting day of a trust established in 1978, which was to vest in 2007.*

The trustee sought an order authorising it to extend the vesting date of the trust, notwithstanding that the variation power in the trust instrument was insufficient to allow such an amendment.

The trustee's reasons for seeking the authorisation included:

(1) *the trust had been established for the intended benefit of the applicant's children and grandchildren, however his adult children were unmarried and without children and unless the application was granted, the trust would vest before his grandchildren could benefit; and*

(2) *the trustee anticipated that capital gains tax of $690,000 and stamp duty of $620,000 would be payable on vesting of the trust, diluting an asset pool valued at approximately $13m.*

The Court granted the order requested as it considered the amendment to be "expedient". The judgment focused primarily on the first reason for the application outlined above, however the dilution to the value of the trust that would have been caused by the capital gains tax and stamp duty costs outlined above were a relevant factor.

A similar sentiment can be found in the Victorian case of Plator Nominees Pty Ltd. *The case involved a trust established in 1972 which had a 40 year vesting period. Consequently the trust was due to vest in 2012.*

The trustee brought an application under s 63A of the Trustee Act 1958 *(Vic) that the vesting day be extended to the date 21 years after the death of the last living relative of one of the primary beneficiaries.*

The trustee's application included the following justifications for the extension:

(1) *the trust was established as a property investment vehicle intended to survive the primary beneficiaries for the benefit of their children, but if it vested in 2012 it would not achieve that purpose;*
(2) *all of the beneficiaries had consented to the extension;*
(3) *no specific reason could be identified as to why 2012 had been nominated as the vesting day; and*
(4) *if the trust vested in 2012 a "significant capital gain" would be realised.*

The Court granted the extension and noted that, consistent with previous judicial authority, the fact that deferral of taxation costs was one of the drivers for requesting the extension did not preclude it from granting the extension.

Re Arthur Brady Family Trust; Re Trekmore Trading Trust arguably further clarifies the position set out in the previous cases.

In that case, the first trust was established in 1977 with a vesting date of 2017. The second trust was established in 2008 with near identical terms to the first trust (presumably as part of a trust 'cloning' arrangement), including the 2017 vesting date.

The applicants sought an order for an extension to the vesting date under the *Trusts Act 1973* (Qld).

The sole reason for the application outlined in the judgment was the applicant's desire to defer capital gains tax and stamp duty costs which would substantially dilute the overall pool of assets to the detriment of the beneficiaries.

The total tax and stamp duty costs across both trusts were anticipated to exceed $1.8m out of an asset pool of $15m.

The applicant submitted that, in order to maintain the property portfolios, the beneficiaries would need to borrow funds to meet the transaction costs. Each of the contingent beneficiaries supported the application.

After a detailed analysis, the Court granted the requested extensions as it was satisfied the "very substantial impact of taxes and duties upon the trust funds" and the unanimous approval of the beneficiaries supported the exercise of its discretion.

Lessons

A few key lessons can be taken from the cases above.

First, many trust deeds from all eras, and particularly those established in the 1970s and 1980s include vesting periods significantly shorter than 80 years.

Practitioners should be alert to this issue and ensure they methodically check the vesting day of every trust as part of any trust dealing.

Secondly, *Re Arthur Brady Family Trust; Re Trekmore Trading Trust* provides authority that the Court may grant an order for the extension of a vesting day even where the sole purpose of the extension is to defer the capital gains tax costs and stamp duty costs that would otherwise arise as a result of the vesting, provided it can be shown that those costs would have a material adverse impact on the beneficiaries.

Finally, although any application to Court carries a degree of risk, recent cases indicate the Court will generally react positively to applications for the extension of vesting dates, where there are compelling commercial or family reasons to order the extension.

Where are we at with trusts?

Posted 10 February 2015

As set out in earlier posts, and with thanks to the Television Education Network, today's post addresses the issue of 'Where are we at with trusts?' at the following link – ***http://youtu.be/ZMgAI9edJ-4***

As usual, a transcript of the presentation for those that cannot (or choose not) to view the presentation is below –

> There's undoubtedly been an enormous amount of hysteria in recent times in relation to trusts generally, but particularly from a family law perspective. That hasn't been helped, because of a series of decisions that have come out from a family law perspective that have got a lot of media attention.
>
> The reality is there's also been an equal number of decisions and pronouncements from the Tax Office across issues, such as unpaid present entitlements, the taxation of trusts generally, resettlements of trusts. So you've had a whole range of things happening under both family law and wider commercial issues that have come out of the courts and out of the revenue offices.
>
> Then on top of that, you've had the government constantly looking to introduce new legislation, and making announcements about what may or may not happen in relation to the taxation of trusts.
>
> These three issues have almost created a perfect storm in terms of the amount of white noise that is around concerning where we are with trusts.

Memos of directions in relation to trusts

Posted 20 October 2015

As set out in earlier posts, and with thanks to the Television Education Network, today's post addresses the issue of memos of directions, or letters of wishes in relation to trusts at the following link –

https://www.youtube.com/watch?v=B9NuAE3lIiM

As usual, a transcript of the presentation for those that cannot (or choose not) to view the presentation is below –

> Memos of directions, or letters of wishes, are a classic example of the 'continuums' that the court has to work in and the overall framework of appropriate public policy.
>
> With letters of wishes, what the courts are generally trying to balance on the one hand, is the idea that they should be there to support the trustees and help them reach the right decision, against the argument that trustees are ultimately responsible to answer to the court and not be subject to anyone else's direction.
>
> Many cases in this area have had factual scenarios where the letters of wishes are referred to in the reasons for a decision by the trustee and the beneficiaries have challenged the decision and directions were sought from the court.
>
> Often, the court will release the letter of wishes and make it known to the beneficiaries. However, the decisions observe that the only reason that the letter of wishes even comes into play is because the trustee chooses to disclose the existence of them.
>
> Therefore, from a planning perspective, it may be a conservative and pragmatic approach that letters of wishes, even if they exist, are not actually disclosed anywhere by the trustee.

Chapter 4

COMPANIES

Can a company own shares in itself?

Posted 8 March 2010

A couple of days ago, a financial adviser and I were looking at helping a client to implement an insurance funded buy-sell arrangement.

Particularly since the downturn over 2008 and 2009, there seems to have been an increasing focus on insurance protection in the context of business succession (quite aside from any keyperson insurance) and we are regularly seeing bank funding approvals being made conditional on the insurance at least covering the bank's lending exposure.

As part of the audit process that we were jointly performing on the client's circumstances, the financial adviser identified that one of the shareholders in the trading company was the trading company itself.

This was not a simple case of the trading company having done some sort of share buyback arrangement – the company was listed under the ASIC records as a one third shareholder in itself.

Although it is an area that is not often considered, the Corporations Act expressly prohibits companies owning shares in themselves and there are a series of practical and (potentially criminal) consequences that can flow.

It looks as though there will be a solution for this client, however as with most breaches of the law, prevention would have been infinitely more palatable than the cure.

How many directors does it take to have a company?

Posted 22 March 2010

Last week, I further explored the issues that came out of a relatively common situation of a loan or unpaid present entitlement owed to a company, where that company was a trading entity.

As mentioned last week, one asset protection strategy that often makes sense on a number of levels is ensuring that the only directors of a trading company are those people who, commercially, absolutely must be a director.

Often, we find situations where, for example, a husband and wife are both directors of a company when only one spouse in fact needs to be.

As directors carry personal liability, this is unnecessarily risky.

While this issue can normally be very easily solved by simply resigning the relevant director and notification to the company and the ASIC, care must be taken.

In particular, all companies, until the late 1990s, had to have at least two directors (and, other than in very limited circumstances, all public companies must still have three directors).

Therefore, even though the Corporations Law has been updated now for about 13 or 14 years now, there are many company constitutions (or as they were formally known as 'memorandum and articles') that still require two directors.

If a director resigns in breach of the company constitution, there can be a series of Corporation Law issues that need to be taken into account. These issues can all be avoided by simply ensuring the company's constitution is updated before the resignation takes place.

When is a share not a share?

Posted 29 March 2010

Special classes of shares have, at least in recent years, always been a hallmark of company structures.

One of the most common descriptions of shares that provide no other rights than simply a dividend at the complete discretion of the directors from time to time is a 'dividend access' or 'dividend only' share.

Last week, we helped an accountant whose client was the subject of a wider ATO audit. For the third time I am personally aware of in the last twelve months, one of the core issues the ATO was pursuing related to the application of the debt equity rules to a purported dividend access share.

For anyone that has spent time considering the debt equity rules, they will know how complex they are (indeed the position paper from the ATO on this point ran to around 15 A4 pages).

The bottom line in a practical sense is if you have clients wanting to implement a dividend access share arrangement and they are not willing to have you provide formal advice about the application (or otherwise) of the debt equity rules, you should get as a minimum confirmation from them that they understand the consequences of a share being treated as debt instead of equity.

More conservatively, you should probably refuse to implement the structure at all, although obviously commercially, this raises a number of difficulties.

For the client last week, if the ATO is successful in arguing that the dividend access share was in fact a debt instrument for tax purposes, it will mean that the 7-digit dividend that had been declared will be completely unfrankable.

Virtual company registers

Posted 9 November 2010

We are seeing an increasing number of accounting firms that we assist with company establishments opt to receive all documentation electronically, as opposed to the traditional provision of a physical folder to store the company register.

The ability to maintain a company register in electronic form only is a relatively recent innovation under the Corporations Act and particularly for accountancy firms who act as registered office for a number of their clients' companies, is certainly one worth exploring.

Obviously, there are a number of issues that always need to be taken into account, however broadly, so long as the following issues are addressed, it should be possible to avoid the need for a physical register to be stored:

(1) The company must resolve that it intends to maintain an electronic, as opposed to a physical, register.
(2) The relevant notification must then be provided to the ASIC.
(3) The company must have a process by which a physical register can be produced if ever required.

ATO attacks Division 7A planning strategy

Posted 21 February 2011

In what is only a slight variation of the Division 7A planning approach of trusts distributing income to a limited partnership, in order to attain a capped rate of tax of 30% and avoid any application of Division 7A on loans made by the limited partnership, the ATO has released a further taxpayer alert last week.

The use of limited partnerships to avoid Division 7A was an approach that the ATO was on record as having concerns about long before the legislation in this area was changed a couple of years ago.

Following the change, a number of advisers were quick to realise that companies limited by guarantee could offer a similar pathway to the limited partnership approach – in other words:

(1) Potentially receive trust distributions, with the tax payable on those distributions capped at the corporate rate of 30%.

(2) The company limited by guarantee could then subsequently make loans that would not, on the face of the legislation, be caught by Division 7A.

In their first taxpayer alert for the year (taxpayer alert TA2011/1), the ATO lists its concerns with the above strategy.

The full alert is set out at the following link – *http://law.ato.gov.au/atolaw/view.htm?docid=%22TPA/TA20111/NAT/ATO/00001%22*.

Keeping it simple with company setups

Posted 3 May 2011

Following the last post, I had a question in relation to how the secretary position of the sole director company was resolved.

Interestingly due to relatively recent changes to the Corporations Act, there is now no longer a requirement to have a secretary for a proprietary limited company.

For those interested to explore the provisions in this regard further, the particular section of the Corporations Act is Section 204A(1).

Financiers being financiers

Posted 14 November 2011

With the continuing economic uncertainty, one area where financiers seem to have had a continued focus on recently is in relation to financial assistance.

Financial assistance can be a relatively complex area of the Corporations Act, however essentially it centres around situations where a company provides some form of help to shareholders (or associates of shareholders) in relation to the provision of finance.

What amounts to financial assistance can be an issue of some debate in many transactions, however ultimately the 'golden rule' invariably applies.

That is a financier will normally have the last word as to whether they believe there is a financial assistance issue.

There is a specific process set out under the Corporations Act that allows a transaction to proceed despite the existence of financial assistance, however there are a number of strict timelines that must be satisfied in order to comply with these provisions. Therefore, unless all parties are aware of the possibility that financial assistance approval may be required, significant difficulties can arise.

What is a ratchet & the Chairman's Red Book

Posted 8 April 2013

The Chairman's Red Book provides a quick reference guide for directors of any company, particularly chairmen of public companies (whether listed or unlisted).

At this stage, the book is only available on request, for anyone interested in receiving a copy, please let me know.

Over the coming weeks, with special thanks to Brett Heading, and the other editors of the publication, there will be posts from the book on some of the core principles featured.

This week's post is shorter than the others (given the background outlined above) and simply answers the question – what is a ratchet.

A ratchet is a mechanism that varies the equity share that management receives on exit, depending on the achievement of certain objectives.

Typically, ratchets are based either on the multiple of money invested that is received on exit after repayment of debt, or the internal rate of return achieved by the private equity fund.

Ratchets can strengthen the alignment of the interests of management and the investor. However, the taxation implications can be complicated and need careful consideration in structuring any agreement.

Deeds of access, insurance and indemnity

Posted 17 April 2013

Following on from last weeks' post, this week's post is again extracted (with thanks) from the Chairman's Red Book.

Under deeds of access, insurance and indemnity, the company usually agrees to:

(1) indemnify the director to the extent permitted by law;
(2) maintain, and pay the premium on a D&O policy covering the director;

(3) maintain a copy of all board papers; and
(4) give the director access to the board papers and other documents of the company.

Access to board papers and company documents is essential for a director to discharge their obligations.

Most companies and directors put in place such agreements on a uniform basis for each director.

Where deeds are required for other executives (non directors) they may require some modification. For example, these officers will typically not be entitled to access the board papers.

D&O exclusions

Posted 24 April 2013

As mentioned in the last post, a D&O policy is normally something that a company should obtain and maintain for each of its directors.

It is important to note however that D&O policies usually exclude cover for acts or omissions of directors, before the policy period commenced, that the director reasonably knew were likely to give rise to a claim and which were not notified to the insurer.

Fraud or dishonesty, or any wilful or deliberate breach of the law by the insured, will also be excluded.

Numerous other standard exclusions are normally set out under a D&O policy.

Although these exclusions are typically 'standard', each company's D&O policy is a bespoke contract and should be checked carefully to understand the coverage limitations.

Gap between indemnity and insurance policy

Posted 30 April 2013

Following on from recent posts, this week's post is again extracted (with thanks) from the Chairman's Red Book.

Given the specific wording of insurance policies and the fact that the deeds of access and indemnity often use general wording, it is clear that there are some forms of liability against which a company will be required to indemnify its directors under the deed of access, insurance and indemnity where the company will not be covered by insurance.

One example is when a director seeks legal advice in anticipation of a claim, which may or may not be made against the director in the future. The D&O policy will only respond to cover legal costs once the claim is made. A gap may also occur because the insurance policy provides cover for a maximum sum whereas the indemnity offered by the company is unlimited.

What is a warranty?

Posted 6 May 2013

Following on from recent posts, this week's post is again extracted (with thanks) from the Chairman's Red Book.

A warranty is essentially a guarantee that a factual statement is correct. Parties will often negotiate to allocate liability for loss between them if the statement turns out to be incorrect.

In a merger and acquisition context, warranties are generally required where a party (often the buyer) makes an assumption when entering into an agreement, and wants to be able to sue the seller if that assumption is incorrect.

For example, where a buyer has determined the purchase price of the target company or business on the basis of its reported earnings, the buyer will usually require the relevant financial statements to be warranted by the seller so that the seller bears the risk of the financial statements being inaccurate.

Warranties are usually 'given' within the sale agreement by the warranting party at the time of entering into the agreement, and repeated at completion. It is also common to see a statement to the effect that the warranties are taken as being repeated each day during the period between signing and completion.

'Standard' warranty limitations include -

(1) Seller's knowledge
(2) Disclosure
(3) Exclude future performance
(4) Buyer's knowledge
(5) Recovery from 3rd parties
(6) Specific (ie provided in the accounts; buyers action post completion; law changes; matter of public record)
(7) Insurance

Indemnities

Posted 14 May 2013

Following on from recent posts, this week's post is again extracted (with thanks) from the Chairman's Red Book.

An indemnity is an undertaking to meet a specific potential liability, or to hold someone 'harmless', on the happening of a particular event, similar to the obligations of an insurer on the happening of an insurable event. Indemnities provide a clear allocation of risk in respect of an event.

The scope of the indemnity provided under an agreement should be carefully considered by the indemnifying party and the trigger for the indemnity clearly understood. Depending on the wording of the indemnity, the amount that is claimable under an indemnity may not be limited by the usual common law requirement of remoteness, or any requirement of the indemnified party to mitigate loss.

Similarly, the indemnity may be open ended and not subject to any limitation or exclusion under the agreement, and in some cases the event need not have been caused by any wrong of the indemnifying party.

Next week's post will look at some of the issues to consider in relation to indemnities.

Things to consider in relation to indemnities

Posted 22 May 2013

The courts have recently applied a restricted view on the use of indemnities and in some cases, have failed to acknowledge the validity of broad, all-encompassing indemnities. Notwithstanding this, claims under clearly expressed indemnities are generally upheld.

The following issues should be considered by anyone providing an indemnity -

(1) the limitation of the loss (i.e. direct loss only and not consequential loss);
(2) the scope of the indemnity (e.g. 'loss in connection with' compared to 'loss caused solely by');
(3) excluding liability under the indemnity where the liability arises as a result of the indemnified party's default or negligence, or limiting it to the extent it has been contributed to by the party;

(4) making the indemnity subject to any exclusions or limitations of liability within the agreement;
(5) requiring the indemnified party to mitigate its loss; and
(6) including a right for the indemnifying party to defend any claim for which it will be liable as a result of the indemnity.

It is common practice for a buyer to request a separate tax indemnity in share sale agreements. This is primarily so that the respective obligations of the parties in relation to tax, including as to timing, are clearly and specifically identified.

It is also common for 'gross up' provisions to be included in these indemnities which account for the tax payable in respect of warranty payments. Consideration should be given to whether it is appropriate for the parties to agree contractually that any warranty payments are to be treated as a reduction of the purchase consideration.

Directors duties

Posted 28 May 2013

Following on from recent posts, this week's post is again extracted (with thanks) from the Chairman's Red Book.

Shareholders have pooled their funds for a common purpose – to conduct an enterprise that they presumably could not afford to conduct on their own. The role of a company director is to guide and grow the business, observing the duties described below.

Chairman have a particular role to lead the board and to establish an environment in which executive management can successfully execute the strategy set for the company by the board.

As those ultimately responsible for the company's actions and the shareholders' funds invested in the company, directors are subject to a strict set of duties, reflecting the position of trust they hold.

An ability to fulfil these duties while successfully growing the business is the mark of a good company director; a clear understanding of risk versus reward is essential.

In summary, directors have the following duties:

(1) act in good faith in the best interests of the company
(2) act for a proper purpose
(3) act with care and diligence
(4) not misuse information they receive in their role, or misuse their position, for their own or someone else's personal gain

(5) avoid conflicts of interest, and
(6) prevent insolvent trading.

Directors' duties have evolved over time. The above duties are now set out in statutes (primarily the Corporations Act), however, a body of case law expands upon the underlying legal and equitable principles. A company's constitution generally also sets out additional duties and obligations of the directors of the company.

As a general rule, directors owe their duties to the company, not the shareholders or creditors of the company. However, there are provisions in the Corporations Act under which a director can be liable to these stakeholders (e.g. liability for insolvent trading).

Chapter 5

POWERS OF ATTORNEY

Should I act as an attorney for a client?

Posted 28 June 2010

A number of people contacted me following last week's post with questions in relation to the consequences of an accountant or financial adviser (or for that matter a lawyer) acting as an attorney for a client.

Many of you will have either professional body guidelines or guidelines that your firm has agreed to implement about the basis on which (if at all) you can take on the role of an attorney.

In a practical sense, the two biggest issues you need to ensure are addressed:

(1) The conflict of interest rules are very strict in this area. It is always preferable to have a very clear statement in the attorney appointment document confirming that the person appointing you as their representative waives any prohibition on you acting due to an issue of conflict.

(2) Similarly, on a number of levels, it is always our strong recommendation that the professional adviser be permitted to charge their standard professional fees. This ability should be clearly set out in the appointment document.

Can an enduring attorney be a company?

Posted 12 July 2010

The issues in relation to attorney appointment over the last couple of weeks have generated a number of questions and comments.

One common theme has been in relation to the distinction between the appointment of an attorney and the role of an executor and/or trustee under a will.

There are a number of distinctions between these various roles, however one of the overriding practical points is that the appointment of an attorney can essentially only be of an individual person.

In contrast, the appointment of an executor or trustee can be of a company or a particular role – for example, you will often see the executor of a will being crafted so that it is the 'senior partner from time to time in the firm of...'

How many powers of attorney does it take to create authority?

Posted 28 February 2011

With increasing regularity, we are seeing issues arise in relation to the authority for people to act under powers of attorney.

Like many laws, the power of attorney legislation is frustratingly inconsistent, with different acts applying in each Australian state.

In theory, there is also legislation requiring each jurisdiction to recognise the documentation prepared in each of the states. In practice, however, it is often extremely difficult to convince third parties that a power of attorney document that looks completely different to what they normally expect to see is in fact legally binding.

One solution (although admittedly not a particularly efficient one) we are seeing more people implement is to have a separate power of attorney prepared under each jurisdiction where they are likely to spend significant periods of time. While not a perfect solution, this approach can provide significant practical benefits.

There is an ongoing push, as part of having uniform succession laws across Australia, for the power of attorney laws to also be made consistent. The timeline for achieving such an outcome is difficult to predict given the number of vested interests involved.

Witnessing powers of attorney

Posted 7 March 2011

Following last week's post, I had a number of people raise concerns about the witnessing requirements for powers of attorney.

Unfortunately, this is yet another example of inconsistencies between each Australian state.

Certainly, in each state, legal practitioners are authorised witnesses for most forms of powers of attorney.

Having this said, documents that are directly related to medical issues can normally only be witnessed by a medical practitioner.

In some states, the financial related power of attorney documents can be witnessed by a relevantly large range of authorised signatories.

Ultimately, as I recommended to the advisers who contacted me, the safest pathway is to carefully read the relevant documentation to ensure all witnessing provisions are complied with. While there are numerous inconsistencies between the various states, each state does at least set out in some detail the witnessing requirement for each document as part of the standard government form.

What are Advanced Health Directives?

Posted 6 August 2012

One issue that comes up relatively regularly in estate planning exercises relates to Advanced Health Directives (**AHD**).

In most jurisdictions, an AHD is essentially a document addressed to a person's medical practitioner setting out the level of care that they would like to receive in a series of specific situations.

Normally, the document is crafted as a 'multiple choice' questionnaire listing out dozens of typical medical scenarios. The document is normally completed in conjunction with a client's GP.

As the document is a medical, not legal, one, most lawyers simply provide access to the standard document rather than providing advice on it.

One important issue to note is that in no Australian state does an AHD create the ability for euthanasia style directions to be articulated.

While a person has legal capacity they may revoke their AHD at any time.

In an upcoming post, we will look at some of the practical difficulties of AHDs.

Difficulties with Advanced Health Directives

Posted 13 August 2012

In last week's post, an overview of Advanced Health Directives (**AHDs**) was provided.

As mentioned in that post, there are a number of significant practical difficulties with AHDs, and in summary, the main issues in this regard include:

(1) The person making the AHD tends to want to be able to have a 'turn off the switch' type provision (or perhaps even euthanasia). No AHD allows this. Unless the donor has specific religious or personal objectives, many of the questions are somewhat irrelevant.

(2) The attitude of a donor when signing the AHD is not necessarily any indication of their attitude in say, ten years time, when the issue arises. Anecdotally many doctors are unwilling to rely on a document from years earlier in the heat of the moment (even if they find that document on an urgent basis).

(3) As the document needs to be completed with a GP it is unlikely that the GP is actually going to be involved in any sort of emergency situation in any event – again, another reason why the doctor actually performing the medical treatment etc, would be very unlikely to either try and find the AHD or even if it is found, look to rely on it.

(4) In contrast, doctors will generally place significant weight on whoever is appointed as the enduring power of attorney. If that enduring power of attorney is also a next of kin and if there is no hint of any dispute in the immediate family group, then the wishes of the person seeking medical treatment will generally be respected.

In next week's post, there will be links provided to the relevant government websites for AHDs in every Australian State.

When can an attorney accept their position?

Posted 22 July 2013

Today's post considers when an attorney may accept their position under an enduring power of attorney (EPA).

This issue was recently considered in DC [2013] QCAT 108. As usual, a full copy of the case is available here –

http://www.austlii.edu.au/au/cases/qld/QCAT/2013/108.html.

In this case, DC had executed an EPA appointing his wife and his son as his attorneys. DC subsequently lost capacity, and his attorneys attempted to use the EPA. However it soon came to light that there were numerous errors in the document, and to remedy this, the attorneys applied to the Queensland Civil Administration Tribunal (QCAT) for a ruling that the EPA was valid.

While there were other issues with the EPA, a key concern was that the son had signed his acceptance as attorney before his father signed the document.

QCAT confirmed that an attorney cannot accept their appointment until an EPA has been executed by the principal who is granting the power in the first place.

Here, QCAT found that given DC had not signed the EPA before his son, no grant of power had been made and therefore the son's purported acceptance was invalid.

QCAT also confirmed however that the invalid acceptance could be remedied by the son simply re-executing the EPA to accept his appointment – and this was possible even though DC had already lost capacity.

Delay in an attorney accepting their position

Posted 20 August 2013

Today's post follows on from the recent post concerning signing of an enduring power of attorney (EPA) and considers the impact of an attorney not accepting their position immediately after the principal executes the document.

The leading case on this point is Whitney v National Australia Bank Ltd [2007] QSC 397. As usual, a full copy of the case is available here –

http://www.austlii.edu.au/au/cases/qld/QSC/2007/397.html.

In this case, Mrs Murphy had executed an EPA in 2003 appointing Mr Whitney and Mr Walker as her attorneys. At some time between 2003 and 2007, Mrs Murphy developed dementia, although there was no question about her capacity at the time of her executing the EPA.

In 2007, the attorneys accepted their position by signing the EPA and shortly thereafter attempted to use it with a bank. The bank refused to accept the EPA, stating that it considered that Mrs Murphy did not have capacity at the time the attorneys signed the EPA.

Mr Whitney applied to the Queensland Supreme Court for a declaration that the attorneys could exercise their powers under the EPA.

The Court confirmed that an attorney may accept their appointment at any time after a principal has validly executed an EPA, even if the principal has since lost capacity, primarily because an EPA is not revoked by a principal's later loss of capacity.

In this case, the acceptance by the attorneys was therefore valid and the costs for the application were imposed on the bank, whose unequivocal refusal to accept the EPA was found to be unjustified.

EPAS and Conflicts of Interest

Posted 29 April 2014

With the aging population, conflicts of interest arising particularly in relation to the use of an enduring power of attorney (EPA) are becoming far more prevalent.

Previous posts have looked at cases like Stanford. Recently we had a client situation that underlined how critical it is to include a conflict of interest provision in an EPA. This style of provision is not standard in any government form and indeed many lawyers do not choose to include such a provision.

The situation the client faced was as follows:

(1) The main asset in the estate was a family home which was owned as joint tenants.

(2) The husband lacked capacity due to advanced dementia, although was otherwise in good health.

(3) Our client (the wife) wanted to include testamentary discretionary trusts under her will to provide for the children of the relationship.

(4) The husband's will was a very basic document and did not allow for testamentary discretionary trusts.

(5) To ensure that half the value of the house would pass into an appropriate structure if the wife predeceased the husband she was wanting to rely on her appointment as the husband's EPA to sever the joint tenancy (for a summary of the distinction between owning assets as joint tenants and tenants in common see ***http://blog.viewlegal.com.au/2010/02/what-exactly-does-jointly-mean.html***).

(6) Due to an appropriately crafted conflict of interest clause in the EPA, the wife was able to quickly and easily implement the severance and avoid some of the more complex solutions that might also have been available such as the unilateral severance of the tenancy or applying for a court ordered will (the court ordered will process is featured in previous posts: ***http://blog.viewlegal.com.au/2013/08/court-drafted-wills.html*** and ***http://blog.viewlegal.com.au/2013/09/using-court-drafted-wills-to-achieve.html***).

EPAs and Gift and Loan Back Arrangements

Posted 6 May 2014

Following the recent post about conflict of interest provisions under an enduring power of attorney (EPA) a question came up as to whether a gift and loan back arrangement would have provided another solution.

A summary of the general way in which a gift and loan back arrangement would work is set out in recent posts (***http://blog.viewlegal.com.au/2014/04/how-gift-and-loan-back-arrangements-work.html***).

The concept raised in the scenario touched on in the recent post was as follows:

(1) The attorney could arrange for a cash gift equal to the value of the husband's interest in the home to a discretionary trust that would ultimately pass to the control of the children of the marriage.

(2) That trust would then lend the amount back to the husband (via his wife as the attorney).

(3) The husband's estate (following his death) would then be required to repay the debt to the trust effectively ensuring that only nominal assets would pass under the husband's will and the main value of the estate would in turn be held via a more robust structure, being the previously established trust.

Obviously the ability to implement this approach would depend entirely on whether the appropriate conflict of interest provision existed under the EPA and whether the attorney could satisfy themselves that they would not be breaching their fiduciary duties to the principal by undertaking the arrangement. There would also be a range of commercial issues that would need to be considered, not least of which the fact that the trust involved would not be a testamentary trust and therefore would not enjoy the various advantages that testamentary trusts have as compared to standard discretionary trusts.

Can an attorney sign a binding nomination?

Posted 6 October 2015

A recent post looked at the issues surrounding SMSF control on trustee incapacity (see – ***http://blog.viewlegal.com.au/2015/07/incapacity-and-smsf-control.html***)

Adviser feedback raised the adjacent issue of whether an attorney can sign a binding death benefit nomination (**BDBN**) on behalf of anincapacitated member.

While there are differing views, there has been at least one decision by the Superannuation Complaints Tribunal confirming that an attorney can make a BDBN, namely Superannuation Complaints Tribunal, Decision D07-08\030. As usual, a link to a full copy of the decision is as follows –

> ***http://www.sct.gov.au/dreamcms/app/webroot/uploads/determinations/D07-08-030.pdf***

The decision of the Tribunal ultimately held the relevant BDBN was invalid for other reasons, it provides at least some authority for the argument that a BDBN need not be made personally by a member.

In this context however it is important to note that the Law Council of Australia, in their submissions to the Australian Law Reform Commission's Report number 124, confirmed its view that some industry funds will not in fact accept nominations made by an attorney.

Generally, at least for self managed funds, it seems to be accepted that an attorney can at a minimum 'affirm' an existing BDBN, if it has lapsed for any reason. This conclusion however is always subject to the terms of the fund's trust deed and a future post will likely consider this aspect in more detail.

Ideally an express power should be included in a member's enduring power of attorney to put the attorney (again subject to the trust deed) in the best position to be able to validly make nominations as they determine appropriate, for example using wording as follows –

a. *Any attorney can enter into transactions where their interests and duty could conflict with my interests in relation to the transaction.*
b. *Any attorney may sign any form of superannuation nomination (whether binding or non-binding, lapsing or non-lapsing) regardless of whether they may be married to or related to or themselves be a nominee.*

Chapter 6

BUSINESS SUCCESSION

Insurance funded buy-sell arrangements

Posted 19 July 2010

Over the last 2 to 3 years, there is rarely a week that goes by where we are not fortunate enough to help a risk adviser implement an insurance funded buy-sell arrangement with their clients.

One issue that comes up surprisingly more regularly than it probably should occurred again last week in relation to the structure of these arrangements.

There is an enormous amount of material on insurance funded buy-sell deeds (if you are interested, spend some time looking at our website – ***www.viewlegal.com.au***).

Invariably, most advisers in this area will, for a multitude of tax and wider commercial reasons, recommend an option based contractual arrangement – these arrangements provide the most amount of flexibility possible for each party.

Where however a discretionary trust is involved in the business structure, it is generally the case under trust laws that the trust deed must expressly permit the granting of options.

The technical reasons for this position revolve around issues concerning the fettering of a trustee's discretion – practically however the position is that unless the trust does have the power to grant options at the date the buy-sell agreement is signed, there is a risk that the agreement may not be enforceable as otherwise anticipated.

ATO ruling on insurance trusts

Posted 7 September 2010

Last week the ATO released a Product Ruling (PR2010/18) in relation to the capital gains tax consequences for the beneficiary of an insurance trust deed.

In many respects the ruling reflects what most specialists in this area (including View Legal) have been saying for many years.

That is that a properly crafted insurance trust deed should provide appropriate protection for the principals of a business without any significant tax detriment, notwithstanding that there may be other commercial issues to consider regarding the structure.

Unfortunately the positive aspects of the ruling are largely undermined by the fact that the outcomes are based on the assumption that the insurance trust deed will create absolute entitlement for each beneficiary in the relevant insurance policy.

As many advisers who work in this area will know, the expressed views of the ATO concerning absolute entitlement are somewhat contentious and the ATO continues to refer to a draft ruling that has never been finalised – despite being issued in 2004.

One practical issue is that the ruling released last week confirms that in order to ensure absolute entitlement the relevant beneficiary must be able to call for the asset at any time.

This largely undermines one of the main reasons advisers had historically recommended insurance trusts – that is that the trustee will have the ability to ultimately control the payment of any insurance proceeds received.

A further practical issue, given the way in which many providers have traditionally structured trust arrangements is that the product ruling only relates to insurance trust deeds where the company acting as trustee is an entity owned and controlled by the principals involved in the business entity and the relevant insurer is not be a party to the arrangements.

For those interested in reading a full copy of the ruling please email me.

Company owned business succession insurance

Posted 22 October 2010

Last week, we revisited with an adviser a strategy that had been put in some years prior by a trading company.

In particular, the trading company had obtained insurance policies for death and permanent disablement over each of the core principals who also controlled the ownership of the shares in the company.

The discussion centered on the tax consequences of a receipt by the company of the insurance proceeds and practically how the transfer of shares to the surviving principals would take place.

While from a simplicity (and Division 7A) perspective, company ownership of business succession insurance can be attractive, the disadvantages do normally outweigh the benefits.

Last week's situation was no different given that on receipt of the insurance pay out by the company, steps would still need to be taken to:

(1) Have the funds transferred to the exiting shareholder or their estate.
(2) Ensure that the exiting shareholder transfers their shares.

As it turns out, primarily due to the significant increase in premiums that would be incurred to rearrange the current ownership structure, the adviser here is looking at other solutions to ensure that the existing structure can work as well as possible. It was however a timely reminder that business succession arrangements do require regular review.

Insurance funded buy-sell arrangements – ATO commentary

Posted 21 March 2011

A number of earlier posts have considered various taxation aspects of insurance funded buy-sell arrangements.

Some minutes recently released from the National Tax Liaison Group meeting towards the end of last year provide an interesting insight to the latest ATO views in this area.

For those who have not seen a full copy of the minutes and would like a copy please email me.

As you will see, in summary:

The status of taxation ruling on absolute entitlement (TR2004/D25) remains unclear.

The ATO considers its finalisation intricately linked to how it will deal with bare trusts, which again remains an unresolved issue.

The ATO confirms that the product ruling released last year in relation to one provider's insurance trust arrangement is based entirely on the assumption that absolute entitlement was created. As my post from last year indicated, this assumption may be an unwise one to make given the ATO's apparent attitude in this area.

While the ATO is flagging that they will further consider providing appropriate guidance, they have specifically confirmed that the Discussion Paper from 2000 on business succession arrangements cannot be considered current.

ATO discussion paper on buy-sell agreements

Posted 28 March 2011

Following last week's post, we had a number of people contact us in relation to the, withdrawn, ATO Discussion Paper on business succession arrangements (i.e. buy-sell agreements).

As mentioned in last week's post, the ATO has unequivocally stated its belief that the Discussion Paper is not current and that advisers in this area should be deterred from relying on it.

This said, the Discussion Paper remains (even 11 years after its initial circulation) the only comprehensive attempt by the ATO to articulate its view of the various business succession models.

For those interested in the issues addressed by the Discussion Paper, please email me.

Please note the copy of the paper I have access to is shown in 'marked up' format as this was the final version released by the ATO before it was withdrawn from circulation.

Insurance funding via superannuation

Posted 24 October 2011

Earlier posts have mentioned the 'debt reduction' and 'hybrid' buy sell arrangements and I can forward information in this regard for those interested.

One particular issue raised with me recently in this area was the ability to use superannuation owned policies for insurance arrangements supporting a debt reduction (or asset protection) solution.

Generally the position is that the asset protection (debt reduction) component of any insurance policy should be self owned, rather than superannuation owned.

This is because a superannuation fund trustee is unlikely to be able to make the required payment directly to the other principals, as the fund can only pay a benefit to a member (in the case of disablement), or to the dependants or estate (in the case of death).

Furthermore, a superannuation fund could not be a party to the agreement as this would raise issues about compliance with the sole purpose test, and also might be construed as an assignment of a benefit, which super fund trustees are prohibited from recognising.

Given these technical limitations, there could be no certainty that insurance proceeds held in superannuation would find their way to the correct parties to enable them to pay down the external debt.

This said, it is often possible to have two policies for each principal under a hybrid buy sell deed, one being a self owned policy for asset protection (debt reduction) purposes and the other policy being owned through superannuation for equity transfer (that is, traditional ownership or buy sell) purposes.

Insurance premiums & FBT

Posted 24 August 2012

As many regular readers would be aware, one particular innovation in recent times in relation to insurance funded business succession arrangements is the so-called 'debt reduction' strategy.

One aspect of the arrangement that is often raised concerns the fringe benefits tax (**FBT**) implications of the premium payments

Broadly, there are a number of reasons as to why FBT will normally not apply to the payment of insurance policy premiums.

Generally the accountant for the business will always be best placed to give the guidance, however some of the reasons FBT will not apply can include –

(1) the arrangements not having anything to do with employment;
(2) in some instances, the otherwise deductible rule; or
(3) while for administrative ease the premiums might be paid by the business, the actual tax position is that the amount is included as part of other payments made (for example, a dividend).

It is important to remember that aside from FBT, there are a number of other tax issues that may also be relevant (for example division 7A or capital gains tax) so it is also best to ensure the exact circumstances are considered by the accountant for the particular client.

Penalising the under insured

Posted 24 September 2012

With thanks to co View Legal director Patrick Ellwood this week's post looks at a situation we had recently under an insurance funded buy sell arrangement where the parties were wanting to craft the agreement in order to penalise a business owner if they were under insured.

In particular there was a desire to ensure that the agreement discounted the purchase price that was otherwise payable under the agreement if the insurance payout was less than the market value of the interest in the business at the relevant date.

For a number of reasons we recommended against this approach, including:

(1) The overall aim of any business succession agreement is to achieve as smooth a transition of the business as possible. If a party to the transaction believes that they are not getting fair value then the prospects of a smooth transmission are significantly decreased.

(2) The exiting owner (or their estate) will still be required to pay tax on the transfer of the interest at full market value (even though the price under the agreement would be less than market value) due to the way in which the market value substitution rules under the Tax Act operate.

(3) Practically, if the exiting party had sold their interest the day before the triggering event, they would have received market value. It is arguably inequitable for an owner to be disadvantaged because of a sudden involuntary exit event, as opposed to a planned voluntary exit.

Generally most agreements (ours included) cater for any shortfall in insurance funding by ensuring that the remaining owners are still required to pay the difference but have an extended period of time (for example, three years) to repay the difference.

Company owned insurance policies for business succession

Posted 4 February 2013

We recently had an adviser seeking more detailed comments about company owned business succession insurance policies.

In particular, feedback was requested about the specific reservations with insurance policies for business succession being owned by a company. In summary, and with thanks to co View Legal director Tara Lucke, we provided the following reasons:

(1) while capital gains tax (CGT) should not be payable on receipt of life insurance proceeds, it will be payable on any total and permanent disablement or trauma proceeds that are paid to a company. In contrast, no CGT should be payable on receipt of the insurance proceeds where the policies are self owned;

(2) there can also be significant practical difficulties in extracting insurance proceeds from a company to the appropriate recipient. This is particularly important when the main purpose of the policy is for an equity payment, as opposed to debt cover. Again, where the policy is self owned, the exiting principal or their estate will receive the proceeds directly and none of these practical issues will arise, as long as an appropriate agreement is implemented;

(3) where insurance proceeds need to be accessed by the exiting principal (or their estate) this is generally only achievable via a share buy-back or dividend. A dividend will likely be tax inefficient and generally a buy back will also have an inefficient tax outcome for the following reasons:

   a the consideration will be split between an assessable capital gain and a dividend, which restricts access to the full benefit of the CGT 50% discount and small business CGT concessions;

   b while a company may be able to pay the proceeds to the exiting shareholder/s as a partially or fully franked dividend, this will use franking credits that would otherwise have been available for distributing profits; and

   c the surviving owner/s will own 100% of a company after a share buy-back, however their cost base in the shares will not have increased;

(4) insurance proceeds will be under the control of the remaining director/s of a company, in contrast with a self owned or superannuation owned policy where the estate directly receives the benefit of the proceeds; and

(5) finally, the legal documentation required for company ownership is comparatively complex to all other policy ownership approaches.

Buy sell deeds, family trusts and the deemed market value substitution rule

Posted 1 July 2013

With thanks to co View Legal director Tara Lucke, today's post considers an issue that has been raised with us by an adviser recently.

It is generally accepted that where a business succession plan is structured with self owned insurance policies and a buy sell deed using put and call options, the deemed market value substitution rules apply for taxation purposes. This outcome occurs notwithstanding that the transfer has been funded (either wholly or partly) by insurance.

Given the recent changes to the rules relating to the taxation of trusts, some uncertainty has arisen in relation to the ability to effectively manage the taxation consequences of a deemed capital gain arising from a transfer under a buy sell deed.

Under the 'interim' taxation rules relating to trusts, there can be particular problems relating to distributions of capital gains arising under the deemed market value substitution rule. In particular, it is generally not possible to create specific entitlement to a deemed capital gain, notwithstanding that there may be a streaming power in the trust deed.

However, where $1 of consideration has been received (which is how we generally recommend buy sell deeds be crafted), provided a beneficiary is made specifically entitled to the $1 of consideration, the deemed gain should be distributed to that same trust beneficiary.

It will therefore be important in each case to consider the specific terms of the trust deed and the other income of the trust, and to craft the distribution minute correctly to ensure the gain can ultimately be distributed to individuals who can access the general 50% capital gains tax discount.

Trust-owned business succession insurance arrangements: Some clarity at long last

Posted 17 March 2015

For those that do not otherwise have access to theWeekly Tax Bulletin, the further article from earlier this month by fellowView LegalDirector Patrick Ellwood and me is extracted below.

Largely due to the level of intergenerational wealth transfer, there has in recent years been an increasing emphasis on all forms of succession planning and, in particular, business succession planning.

In broad terms, a buy-sell agreement is a contractual arrangement between the ultimate owners (or 'principals') of a business. The agreement is structured so that if certain events occur, such as the death or incapacity of a principal, the continuing principals are given the option to purchase the interest of the departing principal.

Most commonly, insurance is obtained to help fund buy-sell arrangements.

Since the withdrawal of the ATO's draft Buy Sell Discussion Paper in 2010 there has been some uncertainty about many aspects of insurance funded buy-sell arrangements, particularly those that utilise insurance trusts.

Recent changes introduced as part of the *Tax and Superannuation Laws Amendment (2014 Measures No 7) Bill 2014* (now awaiting Royal Assent after having been passed by Parliament without amendment) appear to have clarified the position (**the 2015 Changes**).

Trust ownership

The trust ownership approach generally involves the establishment of a special purpose entity, often with an independent trustee appointed, to acquire the insurance policies and then distribute proceeds, on the exit of a principal, in accordance with the terms of the trust instrument.

If the trading entity is itself a trust or owned via a trust (for example, a discretionary trust owning shares in a trading company), then it may not be necessary to establish a separate structure.

The core benefit of an insurance trust is its ability to centralise the ownership of all insurance policies and facilitate the efficient transition of an ownership interest following a triggering event.

Historically, from a tax perspective, the level of uncertainty regarding the tax treatment of the insurance proceeds (compared with that of other ownership models such as self-owned insurance) often undermined the commercial attractiveness of the trust ownership approach.

Certainly an insurance policy taken out by a trustee (who was also the beneficiary of the policy) over one or more principals, was likely to see the proceeds paid directly to the trustee and be exempt from CGT pursuant to s 118-300 of the ITAA 1997.

However, due to a lack of guidance from the ATO, many advisers believed there was a risk CGT was triggered where a new principal joined the business and there was any change to the trustee or insurance policy or on the subsequent distribution of the insurance proceeds to the beneficiary.

The concerns were largely driven by the ongoing uncertainty around the concept of 'absolute entitlement', discussed later in this article.

2010 ATO ruling

The ATO released Product Ruling PR 2010/18 in relation to the CGT consequences for the beneficiary of what is generally seen as a 'standard' insurance trust deed.

In many respects, the ruling reflects what most specialists in this area have advised for many years, namely, that a properly crafted insurance trust deed should provide appropriate protection for the principals of a business without any significant tax detriment, notwithstanding there might be other commercial issues to consider regarding the structure.

Unfortunately, the positive aspects of the ruling were largely undermined by the fact that the outcomes are based on the stated assumption that the insurance trust deed will in fact create 'absolute entitlement' for each beneficiary in the relevant insurance policy.

As has been widely documented, the expressed views of the ATO concerning absolute entitlement are somewhat contentious and the ATO continues to refer to a draft ruling that has never been finalised – despite being issued in 2004 (ie Draft TR 2004/D25).

In this regard, a significant concern was that the Product Ruling confirmed that, in order to ensure absolute entitlement, the relevant beneficiary must be able to call for the asset at any time. This largely undermined one of the main commercial reasons why advisers historically recommended insurance trusts, being that the trustee will be able to control the payment of any insurance proceeds received.

A further practical issue, given the way in which many providers traditionally structured trust arrangements, was that the Product Ruling only related to insurance trust deeds where the company acting as trustee was an entity owned and controlled by the principals involved in the business entity and the relevant insurer was not a party to the arrangements.

ATO minutes

Minutes released from a National Tax Liaison Group meeting in December 2010 (item 9) provided further insight into the apparent ATO views in relation to insurance trust deeds.

In summary the minutes stated:

a the status of the taxation ruling on absolute entitlement (Draft TR 2004/D25) is unclear;
b the ATO considers the finalisation of Draft TR 2004/D25 as intricately linked to how it will deal with bare trusts, which again remains an unresolved issue;
c the ATO believes that the Product Ruling released in relation to one provider's insurance trust arrangement is based entirely on the assumption that absolute entitlement was created. This assumption might be an unwise one to make, given the ATO's apparent attitude in this area; and
d while the ATO flags that it will further consider providing appropriate guidance, it specifically confirmed that the ATO Buy Sell Discussion Paper is not current.

Ultimately, given the complexities in this area and the uncertainty created by the ATO Buy Sell Discussion Paper, Draft TR 2004/D25, the Product Ruling and the above minutes, many advisers defaulted to recommending the obtaining of a private ruling on any proposed trust arrangement documenting an insurance funded buy-sell agreement from the ATO before implementing the approach.

Needing to seek a private ruling on what was otherwise a relatively benign arrangement was for many business owners sufficient reason to either use a different ownership approach or, more commonly, simply decide against implementing a business succession plan.

The 2015 changes

Amongst other amendments, the 2015 changes have adjusted the way insurance payments are taxed in certain circumstances.

In particular, the 2015 changes amend the ITAA 1997 to:

(1) remove the requirement that, in order to access the exemption under s 118-300, the insurance proceeds are received by the original 'beneficial' owner of the life insurance policy. The amendment removes the reference to 'beneficial' to clarify that a trustee is eligible for the exemption, where they hold the beneficial interest in the policy for a beneficiary;
(2) extend the exemption for compensation for injury/illness (ie total and permanent disablement and trauma insurance proceeds) in s 118-37 to apply where the proceeds are received by the trustee of a trust or superannuation fund (subject to certain policy ownership prohibitions for superannuation funds), if the injured/ill person is a beneficiary of the trust; and
(3) insert a CGT exemption where a trustee makes a payment to a beneficiary (or their legal personal representative) in respect of life, TPD or trauma insurance proceeds. This change also ensures that where the relevant trust is a unit trust, CGT event E4 does not apply.

The 2015 changes make it likely that trust and superannuation fund ownership of life, total and permanent disablement or trauma insurance policies will be more attractive, given the new clarity regarding the tax treatment of the insurance proceeds.

Importantly, the changes also operate to reflect the intended administrative position of the ATO in this area, and therefore apply from 1 July 2005 and taxpayers adversely impacted who would otherwise be out of time are granted an extension to amend their returns.

Chapter 7

STRUCTURING

What exactly does 'jointly' mean?

Posted 22 February 2010

On three separate occasions last week, the issue of 'jointly' owned assets arose.

A concise summary of the difference between owning something as joint tenants and tenants in common can be found via the 'learn' and then 'resources' tabs of the View Legal website (www.viewlegal.com.au).

Practically, the distinction normally becomes most relevant at times when it is too late to implement a change – for example on death, litigation or relationship breakdowns.

As a general rule (although there are always exceptions), for most business owners, professionals or people in long term relationships, jointly owned assets should be owned as 'tenants in common' to provide the greatest amount of flexibility. This conclusion is not always the case and in fact often the preferred position is that one party has no ownership of the relevant asset – in other words, as part of the review process, it is transferred to another person or structure.

Ultimately, as I was reminded last week, there are two things you should keep in mind, namely:

Remember the distinction between the two joint ownership structures.

Make sure that in relation to each asset for any particular client, you know which ownership structure applies.

UPEs and an asset protection trap

Posted 1 March 2010

Understandably, there has been enormous amount of literature published in recent times concerning the attitude of the ATO in relation to unpaid present entitlements (UPE).

This week I had a timely reminder that while those tax driven issues are critical, they are in fact not as important as the underlying loan or UPE itself.

In particular, I was helping an accountant who had a client whose trading company had been served with litigation proceedings. My role was to help review all structures in the group from an asset protection perspective, although as the litigation lawyer here politely reminded us (I do not get involved in any actual court work if I can avoid it), it was probably not the most opportune time to be doing the asset protection audit.

In any event, while the overall structure of the group was fairly sensible, there was one, very large, asset on the trading company's balance sheet. That asset was a UPE (or if the ATO chooses to ignore industry feedback and finalises its draft ruling – a loan) owed to the trading company by a passive investment trust.

Despite bankruptcy clawback rules, there may be a solution for this client that we are currently exploring. The situation they have to address, now urgently, is of course less than ideal and was a timely reminder that all clients should be encouraged to undertake an asset protection 'audit' regularly.

Next week (or if another more relevant topic arises, within the next few weeks), I will relay one other difficulty with this client's structure that is likely to not be able to be addressed – but could have been with some forward planning.

Trustee companies and specialisation

Posted 26 July 2010

Today's post relates to an asset protection issue that unfortunately is too often overlooked.

Many will have heard lawyers referring to the 'domino theory'.

This theory is one of the very basic asset protection concepts of ensuring that there is a deliberate limit placed on the number of assets owned by any one entity. Furthermore, the assets owned by a particular entity should be of comparable risk profiles.

A similar issue arises in a slightly different context where a company acts as trustee for a trust. In this situation, while the company will be the legal owner of all assets of the trust, it will not have beneficial ownership.

In a number of instances recently, we have seen situations where the trustee company does in fact own assets in its own right, even if this is simply cash, unpaid entitlements or at call loans.

In these situations, those assets are unnecessarily exposed to difficulties that might be encountered by the trust.

In order to maximise the trustee company structure, care must always be taken to ensure that its assets are no more than the initial capital paid up on establishment of the company (i.e. $2).

Next week, we will look at the specific scenario today's post was inspired by, that being a trustee company that had also been used for many years as the corporate beneficiary for the trust.

Trustee companies multitasking

Posted 2 August 2010

Last week we touched on the importance of trustee companies not accumulating assets in their own right.

The specific example that inspired last week's post related to a recent client situation where the trustee company had been used to receive distributions out of the trust that it acted as trustee for.

Often advisers assume that it is not in fact possible at law for a trustee company to also act as the corporate beneficiary. While this is often a good assumption, it is not necessarily the case.

The question of whether a trustee company can in fact be a beneficiary of the trust it acts as trustee for depends on the terms of the trust deed.

Even where a trustee company is listed under the trust deed as a potential beneficiary of the trust that it acts as trustee for, we normally strongly recommend against it being used as a corporate beneficiary.

This is because the trustee is liable for any difficulties that arise against the trust.

It is therefore preferable a completely 'cleanskin' company acts as the corporate beneficiary in order to ensure that the accumulated profits of the trust are quarantined from any litigation against the trustee from time to time.

Trustee indemnity case – appeal

Posted 29 November 2010

Even though the post last week touched on a court case that was relatively widely reported, the importance of the streaming decision meant I felt it appropriate to profile.

This week another court decision caught my eye, even though it was simply in relation to the granting of leave to appeal a previous decision.

Many readers will have noticed the 'Bruton Holdings' case from earlier in the year. In that case, a single court judge held that a corporate trustee was not indemnified by a trust for expenses incurred in (successfully) challenging the Tax Office.

The lack of indemnity was largely based on the fact that the expenses were incurred after it had ceased to be trustee of the trust.

An appeal has now been granted against the original decision on the basis that -

a. the issues are of general importance to the powers and rights of trustees; and
b. the state of the law regarding the powers and rights of bare trustees is not settled.

Business licences

Posted 16 May 2011

The combination of the Bamford decision and the Tax Office's attitude in relation to unpaid present entitlements have meant that we have spent a significant amount of time recently looking at optimal structures for business and investment purposes.

One approach that we have seen an increasing number of clients and advisers consider where a business is owned by a discretionary trust, is the licensing of that business to a trading company.

Obviously, there are a number of tax and stamp duty issues that need to be considered in relation to this approach.

A recent case however seems to confirm that at least in relation to the philosophical legal questions, this kind of approach is now available.

For those who are interested to learn more, a copy of the decision is at the link below. One of the most important paragraphs in the decision is number 42, which highlights the distinction between a goodwill licence and a business licence.

http://www.austlii.edu.au/au/cases/sa/SASC/2010/279.html

Why do so many people still talk about Richstar?

Posted 31 October 2011

The interest for the last couple of posts about accessing assets of a family trust on marriage breakdown reminded me of the Richstar decision.

It has been a few years since the very well publicised decision in Richstar was handed down. The decision does however remain an interim one and there does not seem to be any clear indication as to if or when proceedings might be recommenced.

For those unfamiliar with the exact decision of Richstar, please email me and I can provide a summary.

While there had been a number of cases that have criticised various aspects of Richstar, it still seems to be generally the case that most commentators strongly recommend that the broad principles in Richstar be considered as part of any trust structuring exercise (whether it be the establishment of a new trust or the variation of a pre-existing trust).

Pragmatically, it may also be that part of the reason that Richstar has remained so relevant despite the fact that it is only an interim decision of a single judge from Western Australia is that the judge involved became the Chief Justice of the High Court in 2008.

No removal of business duty in Queensland

Posted 24 January 2012

Today's post summarises an important issue for anyone conducting business in Queensland.

In particular, the Queensland government has announced in its January 2012 interim budget, the deferral of its plan to abolish transfer duty on non-land Queensland business assets.

Broadly, business assets include goodwill, valuable contractual rights, trade debtors, plant and equipment.

The deferral is 'until the budget can accommodate the abolition' –which many commentators are assuming will be indefinitely.

The abolition had been scheduled from 1 July 2013, following the original aim to see it removed on the introduction of GST in July 2000.

As many readers will be aware, other jurisdictions have either abolished duty on non-land business assets (e.g. Victoria, Tasmania and ACT) or have scheduled to abolish it.

PPSA and company charges

Posted 27 February 2012

The long awaited transition to the personal property security regime has continued to evolve since the official 'live' date of 30 January 2012.

While there are an ever increasing number of war stories, for anyone involved in advising companies, arguably one of the most tangible changes has been the abolition of ASIC forms in relation to registering company charges.

Today's post focuses on some of the critical aspects of the new company charge regime.

On 30 January 2012, ASIC ceased to register company charges and ASIC forms 309, 311 and 312 are no longer relevant.

No forms – The difference between the PPS register and the ASIC register of company charges is that there are no physical forms that are lodged with the PPS register. All registrations, amendments and releases are done online using the PPS register (i.e. no forms are signed).

How do I find out if a company has charges against its assets? –ASIC searches will no longer show details of current registered charges. You will need to search the PPS register to reveal these details. As the PPS register search function has experienced a number of technical difficulties, you should always search a company by ACN, ABN and company name until these issues are resolved.

How do I register a security interest? –In order to register a security interest on the PPS register you need to register a financing statement.

How do I release a security interest? –As the ASIC form 312 is no longer relevant, parties will need to agree on a way to document the release in another fashion e.g. a deed of release.

Valuations for the small business CGT concessions

Posted 4 June 2012

There have been a number of court decisions in recent times focused on the way in which valuations are conducted for the purposes of satisfying (what is currently) the '$6M net asset test' for the small business capital gains tax concessions.

The Tax Office has recently released a Decision Impact Statement following one of the cases from last year (for a full copy of the statement, please email me).

In the statement the Tax Office has confirmed that its publication 'market valuation for tax purposes' provides the guidance that it believes should be followed in order to establish a market value for tax purposes.

In particular, the Tax Office states that it believes market value should be determined with reference to the 'highest and best use' of each asset being assessed.

While generally the sale price of an asset will be its market value, the Tax Office believes that each situation must be considered on a case by case basis to determine the most appropriate methodology for determining market value.

Often this will lead to reference to the long standing concept of 'what a desirous buyer would have paid as a fair price to a willing vendor who was not necessarily desirous (or over anxious) to sell'.

What are some of the advantages of a professional partnership incorporating?

Posted 1 October 2012

As set out in earlier posts, and with thanks to the Television Education Network, today's post addresses the issue of 'What are some of the advantages of a professional partnership incorporating?'. If you would like a link to the video please let me know.

As usual, a transcript of the presentation for those that cannot (or choose not) to view the presentation is below –

The biggest thing I guess with incorporation is that, if only from a perception perspective, but in reality from many other perspectives as well, the ability to facilitate the entry and exit is significantly easier.

Probably the greatest example of that is in relation to transaction costs. In most Australian states already – and in those that haven't done it, it's not very far away – there has been the abolishment of stamp duty on the transfer of shares in unlisted companies.

So what that means in a very practical sense is that shares can be moved without any immediate transaction costs between current owners and future owners. That obviously significantly simplifies and reduces the transaction costs that would otherwise be involved.

Conceptually as well, the ability to create employee share type arrangements or have partial sell downs is significantly easier in a corporate environment than it has historically been in a trust environment, or if there's individual partners involved.

In relation to the stamp duty side of things, it is an important consideration to take into account. Basically every Australian state now has abolished stamp duty. Victoria and Tasmania actually led the way originally by abolishing stamp duty on transfers of unlisted shares. The only major Australian state now that hasn't done it is New South Wales and the government has released a timetable that would see the abolishment of that duty very soon.

'Deriving' trust income

Posted 8 October 2012

This week's post looks at a recent case from the Federal Court and is of interest for those following the ongoing debate about trust income.

The name of the case was *SCCASP Holdings as trustee for the H&R Superfund v FCT* (a link to the full copy of the decision is as follows –

http://www.austlii.edu.au/cgi-bin/sinodisp/au/cases/cth/FCA/2012/1052. html?stem=0&synonyms=0&query=SCCASP%20Holdings%20\).

In summary, the core factual background was as follows:

(1) A family trust that had made a capital gain of $14 million sought to have this received by a related self managed superannuation fund (**SMSF**).
(2) The ATO was seeking to argue that in the hands of the SMSF, the income was 'special income' and therefore taxed at 47%, as opposed to the taxpayer who argued that it was only subject to tax at the standard income tax rate for SMSFs (namely 15%).
(3) The particular 'technical' argument that the taxpayer sought to rely on was that because the trustee of the family trust had not made a decision to pay or apply any amount of the capital gain, then for the purposes of the tax rules, it could not be said that the SMSF 'derived' the income.

Ultimately, the Court agreed with the Tax Office and held that the word 'derived' extended to effectively capture anything that was ultimately received by the SMSF, and in particular, extended to the concepts such as money being 'attributed' or 'imputed' to the SMSF.

What are some of the issues with a professional partnership 'rolling over' into a company structure?

Posted 11 February 2013

As set out in earlier posts, and with thanks to the Television Education Network, today's post addresses the issue of 'What are some of the issues with a professional partnership 'rolling over' into a company structure?' at the following link –

http://youtu.be/pIwVOyEAeBA

As usual, a transcript of the presentation for those that cannot (or choose not) to view the presentation is below –

The rollover at face value is always the easiest way to go, because it removes one seriously significant transaction cost being the capital gains tax implications. The problem though is that when you dig a little bit deeper, that is a little illusionary at times, particularly for a group of individual partners rolling over to a company. The attraction of taking that style of rollover can be diminished by the fact that they will still individually own the shares in the company.

So if it's a standard rollover, for example a partnership to a company under Division 122B of the Tax Act, ultimately, the individuals would still actually own the shares in the company. What they will have done is taken away 100 cents in the dollar, if that's the right way to say it, of income that they've historically been enjoying and replaced that with 70 cents in the dollar and an imputation credit or franking credit.

This can lead to a situation where people, having done a rollover are then looking to restructure again anyway. So effectively it's a double restructure because they'll want to divest themselves individually of shares and make those shares be owned via some sort of discretionary trust arrangement.

It can also lead into a range of other potential restructures, dividend access shares and these types of arrangements that certainly get away from the overall goal in the first place, which was to simplify arrangements and get true limited liability.

The other areas (and some of these touched on in other parts of today's program) that obviously need to be taken into account include that while there is no stamp duty on unlisted shares, there is certainly stamp duty in every state moving from an individual or partnership arrangement into a company arrangement.

That's a significant transaction cost that cannot be avoided in any way, shape or form currently and needs to be paid upfront effectively to get yourself into the new structure.

The other ancillary costs that go around an incorporation include issues such as payroll tax, which is inevitably a lot more expensive if you've moved into a company structure as opposed to remaining in a partnership structure.

How do business, or goodwill, licences work?

Posted 19 February 2013

As set out in earlier posts, and with thanks to the Television Education Network, today's post addresses the issue of 'How do business, or goodwill, licences work?'. If you would like a link to the audio please let me know.

As usual, a transcript of the presentation for those that cannot (or choose not) to listen to the presentation is below –

The key idea, and it's probably not dissimilar to some sort of service trust arrangement, is having the two arms of the business being conducted by different entities.

An example, particularly for those that are currently in a partnership of individuals is that if the right to run the business was able to be utilised by someone else or by another entity, for example a partnership of trusts, then there's arguably the ability to create a licence arrangement that would say that the partnership of trusts has the ability to do everything to conduct the business and to enjoy the fruits of conducting the business, the income that's generated for the payment of invariably a relatively nominal fee back to the actual original owners of the business.

Now the idea of that arrangement obviously, particularly from an asset protection perspective is that, if you can get the risks associated from running the business away from the individuals, that's obviously a very attractive thing.

It also gives the partners the ability to think a little bit strategically about how they would want that income derived. So in other words, rather than earning the income in their own name, they have the ability to earn it through a company or trust environment.

How should a partnership of discretionary trusts be structured?

Posted 19 March 2013

As set out in earlier posts, and with thanks to the Television Education Network, today's post addresses the issue of 'How should a partnership of discretionary trusts be structured?' by way of audio podcast (not video) at the following link –***http://youtu.be/qPJJ_1NRwcw***

As usual, a transcript of the presentation for those that cannot (or choose not) to listen to the presentation is below –

There's a number of aspects relevant here.

The biggest one, if we pick up on that idea of it being a little bit of a messy structure, is that ideally there should be some sort of corporate entity that's the face to the outside world. We see that being used very regularly.

Now whether that's a standalone nominee or agent company that's appointed to act on behalf of all the trusts or whether in fact you just have one company acting as trustee for all of the trusts is probably a mute point.

The outcome that's delivered to the outside world is that they're not having to deal with numerous separate trusts; as far as the clients know, all they see is that standalone Pty Ltd company. That would probably be the biggest thing.

The other types of things that need to be thought about I guess are looking at the constitution of that company and making sure that you've got an appropriate balance between directorship powers and shareholder powers.

You'd also obviously, particularly if you're going to use the same company as trustee for a number of trusts, need to have a fairly good understanding of how an appointor or principal or nominee type power under the trust documents work, to give everyone the comfort of knowing that they do have ultimate say over 'their' particular trust.

Probably, the final point would be, and we've got recurring themes coming through here, (this harks back to this concept of asset protection) that is, if you're serious about maintaining protection against issues that might go wrong in the practice, it would really be quite important in our view that the trust that is involved as a partner in the partnership of trusts do nothing else but be a partner in that partnership.

So in other words, you don't buy the investment property in that trust and you don't have a listed share portfolio in that trust, because otherwise you're potentially exposing all those passive assets to the risks of the business.

Why would a professional partnership incorporate?

Posted 26 March 2013

As set out in earlier posts, and with thanks to the Television Education Network, today's post addresses the issue of 'Why would a professional partnership incorporate?'. If you would like a link to the audio please let me know.

As usual, a transcript of the presentation for those that cannot (or choose not) to listen to the presentation is below –

The number of answers to this question are probably only limited to the number of professional practices there are out there. There are a range of reasons.

Tax is one and we keep coming back to that, but that can sometimes be in the eye of the beholder from that perspective.

We're seeing, certainly from a risk management perspective and asset protection and the credit crunch and everything else that's going on and the changes to the bankruptcy rules in the recent past mean that everyone is much more aware that when things go wrong, it's very attractive to have your liability limited.

Obviously, that's probably the biggest advantage of an incorporated model.

There's also I guess the sense from people talking about retaining key staff and the skills shortage that many professional organisations are facing these days that it tends to make sharing of equity a lot easier if you've got a true corporate model.

That can sometimes be as simple from a perception viewpoint that a lot of times staff or key employees are much more aligned and find it much easier to understand a company setup as opposed to some sort of fancy trust arrangement or a service trust arrangement for that matter.

Certainly, the transaction costs side of things, in terms of the hard costs, particularly stamp duty, in most states now, the concept of having to pay stamp duty on the transfer of listed shares is basically a thing of the past. So that can be very attractive to people.

The last main reason and perhaps this is touching on the perception side of it again, I think the corporate model from a governance perspective, it tends to be a lot easier for people to understand.

We've done a lot of work in this area and it is interesting that by becoming a director, and by having a board and by having shareholders and all of these sorts of more formal things, even though the deck chairs haven't really changed in the organisation, there seems to be an air of governance around the place that just wasn't there while they remained as a partnership.

What are the broad alternatives for professionals not wanting to use service trusts?

Posted 3 April 2013

As set out in earlier posts, and with thanks to the Television Education Network, today's post addresses the issue of 'What are the broad alternatives for professionals not wanting to use service trusts?'. If you would like a link to the video please let me know.

As usual, a transcript of the presentation for those that cannot (or choose not) to view the presentation is below –

There's the ability to completely restructure the existing arrangements and move into a new structure and if that alternative was to be taken, there are then a series of different arrangements that might be entered into, and that can include a new structure in total, or some sort of hybrid arrangement.

The types of structures that are available are only really limited by your imagination in terms of what may or may not be useful.

Obviously, there are also a number of commercial issues that need to be taken into account. Many of those will be driven by the actual underlying nature of the partnership that's involved, but generally there are two alternatives if you're moving out of an individual structure, and that can be to incorporate or to form some sort of trust arrangement.

Within those two parameters or those two goalposts, there's quite a large playing field in terms of what that might look like. So in some instances, there's a hybrid between both companies and trusts. In other instances, there are trusts which are of a hybrid nature. So in other words, a unit trust or some sort of partnership of trusts or a blended discretionary trust. Again the common theme is that it's largely driven by what's going to be most useful for the underlying partners involved.

What are the main advantages and disadvantages of using a partnership of discretionary trusts for a professional practice?

Posted 10 June 2013

As set out in earlier posts, and with thanks to the Television Education Network, today's post addresses the issue of 'What are the main advantages and disadvantages of using a partnership of discretionary trusts for a professional practice?' at the following link – ***http://youtu.be/AzNQv_QLMd4***

As usual, a transcript of the presentation for those that cannot (or choose not) to view the presentation is below –

I'll start with the advantages and there are many. Probably the biggest one is the access to the small business concessions moving forward.

Again as we've touched on in other parts of today's program, the ability for a partnership of trusts for each individual partner to gain access to the small business concessions is one that just simply cannot be ignored.

Obviously, discretionary trusts are the vehicle of choice by and large for most small to medium sized businesses these days. So the ability to combine both the small business concession access with individual autonomy and flexibility on income tax planning is very attractive.

The other issue I guess with a partnership of discretionary trusts is that it's relatively simple to explain and understand. This point is often in the eye of the beholder and we'll talk in a moment about some of the disadvantages and how this same advantage can in fact be a disadvantage, particularly in larger practices.

This issue can often be managed by making sure that the one company is trustee for all trusts in the group, and also perhaps acting as a nominee to the outside world, so that as far as clients are concerned, they are in fact only dealing with one entity, being the corporate trustee of a number of different trusts.

The final point to make however in relation to the advantages is that the ability to limit liability to the actual interest in the practice is solely dependent on the actual trust making sure that it only owns one asset, being it's interest in the partnership.

So in other words, the attraction of perhaps having different assets inside that one structure very much diminishes the ability to limit liability in relation to issues that might arise.

The disadvantages are probably not dissimilar to the advantages, just looking at things from the other side of the fence obviously. I touched on in the advantages that the ability to have a number of partners in partnership via the trust structure can be an advantage.

Obviously, it can be a disadvantage as well, and particularly as partnerships get bigger, the concept of having countless discretionary trusts involved can administratively be quite prohibitive. Now argument would be that as long as you have the same corporate trustee across the group, that can be attractive.

This of itself creates further issues, particularly from a control perspective, because you then need to have the individual trusts looking very carefully at issues such as the appointorship, to make sure that if there is disharmony within the partnership that there's an exit mechanism, via the trusts, for each of the individual partners.

Conceptually also, while the attraction of the small business concessions is very strong, you are not getting away from the stamp duty costs.

So in other words, if an individual trust decides to dispose of its partnership interest, it will still very much be exposed to all of the normal stamp duty costs at an ad valorem rate, on the full unencumbered value of interest in the partnership.

The last point, and this is in direct contrast to what the situation is for companies, is that you do not really have a corporate model.

So all of the normal advantages that you associate with incorporation, such as employee share arrangements, become very difficult indeed to achieve, because you've got this disparate structure of a number of different trusts involved in relation to the partnership.

Stamp duty on changes of trustee

Posted 17 September 2013

One issue that is coming up increasingly regularly is changing trustees of either family trusts or self managed superannuation funds.

Generally, there are no tax consequences on the change of trustee for any form of trust (including a superannuation fund).

In each Australian State, there are also provisions that provide a stamp duty rollover on the change of trusteeship.

Care must always be taken however to review at least two issues from a stamp duty perspective.

Firstly, care must be taken to ensure that the correct state law is being applied. There can be complications in this regard where a trust is setup under one jurisdiction, but it has substantial assets in another state.

Once this threshold issue has been resolved, the exact provisions of the relevant stamp duty legislation need to be considered. While each state has similar provisions, there are differences. One example in this regard is that in New South Wales (among other things), any new trustee cannot be a potential beneficiary under the terms of the trust.

Share self-ownership – a structuring warning

19 November 2013

For those that do not otherwise have access to the Weekly Tax Bulletin, the article from last week is extracted below.

Recent articles in this *Bulletin* (for example, 2013 WTB 38 [1642] and WTB 43 [1821]) have focused on the various issues that can arise in relation to the use of corporate beneficiaries by discretionary trusts.

A separate issue that practitioners must be aware of whenever reviewing existing structures or establishing new entities, arises under the *Corporations Act 2001*. In particular, the Act expressly prohibits companies from owning shares in themselves.

This can arise in instances where a trustee company is incorrectly established with the trust (for which it is trustee) owning some or all of the shares. As the legal owner of those shares is the trustee, this results in the trustee owning shares in itself.

The relevant section is s 259A, which provides as follows:

"A *company must not acquire shares (or units of shares) in itself except:*

a *in buying back shares under section 257A; or*
b *in acquiring an interest (other than a legal interest) in fully-paid shares in the company if no consideration is given for the acquisition by the company or an entity it controls; or*
c *under a court order; or*
d *in circumstances covered by subsection 259B(2) or (3).*"

Under s 259F of the Act, if a contravention has occurred, a person who was involved (which is widely defined and includes any person who was, directly or indirectly, knowingly concerned in or party to the contravention) in the contravention may be subject to a civil penalty of up to $200,000. There are also potential criminal consequences that can flow from the breach.

Due to the potentially significant penalties that can arise under the Act, together with the likely adverse commercial ramifications, any identified breach of s 259A should be remedied as soon as practical following identification of the issue.

One option is for the persons involved in the contravention to apply to ASIC for a no-action letter, whereby ASIC confirms it does not intend to take any steps as a result of a particular contravention of the Act.

As flagged above, a breach of the Act in the SME space most typically arises where a trustee company of a family discretionary trust is listed under ASIC records as having its shares owned by the trust. That is, the trustee of the trust owns shares in itself. While "circular" ownership arrangements can be beneficial from an asset protection perspective, they must still comply with the Act.

The preferred approach therefore, where the shares in a corporate beneficiary are to be owned by a trust, is for a structure along the following lines:

(1) the shares in the corporate trustee should be owned by individuals with a low risk profile;
(2) the corporate trustee should undertake no activities other than its trusteeship and the value of the shares in the trustee company should therefore be limited to their issue price; and
(3) the trustee company in its capacity as trustee should own all of the shares in the corporate beneficiary.

What constitutes dutiable value of a transaction?

Posted 27 January 2015

With thanks to team member Hayden Dunnett, today's post looks at the High Court decision in Commissioner of State Revenue v Lend Lease Development Pty [2014] HCA 51. The decision As usual, a full copy of the decision is available via the following link ***http://www.austlii.edu.au/au/cases/cth/HCA/2014/51.html***.

In most jurisdictions, when a dutiable transaction such as a transfer of land occurs, duty is charged on the greater of the consideration or the unencumbered value of the land.

The Lend Lease transaction involved a complex multistage development between Lend Lease and the Victorian Urban Development Company ("Vic Urban"). Part of the development agreement included Lend Lease purchasing seven parcels or land, and in addition, making four payments for various infrastructure and service costs relating to the parcels of land.

The Commissioner argued the dutiable value of the transfer of each parcel of land to Lend Lease included the additional payments. Lend Lease on the other hand thought the consideration stipulated in the contract of sale for each transfer of the land was the dutiable proper amount.

The Court found in favour of the Commissioner, determining that what was received by Vic Urban was stipulated in the development agreement as a 'single, integrated and indivisible' transaction rather than in separate contracts of sale. Duty was therefore payable on the additional payments made by Lend Lease.

The decision confirms that there may be situations where the dutiable value of the transaction may be greater than the payment made for the asset itself.

Where a transfer is one part of a wider transaction, the transaction in its entirety should be considered to determine if any collateral agreements need to be included in determining the dutiable value of the transaction.

Chapter 8

SUPERANNUATION

Superannuation death benefits

Posted 31 January 2012

The way in members of a super fund can direct payment of benefits on death come up in virtually every estate planning exercise.

Essentially a member of a superannuation fund has three main choices for specifying what should happen in relation to their superannuation entitlements on death (assuming the proposed recipient is entitled at law), namely:

(1) nomination – the trustee is bound to deal with a member's benefit in their best interests. The trustee will normally make enquiries as to the member's family situation, who their dependants are, the provisions of their will and other relevant circumstances before making a decision;

(2) a non-binding nomination – the trustee is not bound by a non-binding notice and has an absolute discretion as to where the death benefit will be paid. Where a non-binding notice is made, it should be taken into account as part of any decision by the trustee as to how to distribute the benefit; or

(3) a binding nomination – the trustee is obliged to distribute a member's death benefits in accordance with a valid binding notice.

Binding nominations have the potential to allow members to protect their death benefits from disputes, as where there is no nomination or a non binding one, a trustee's decision can be challenged. Binding nominations can also be used as part of a member's overall estate plan, including, for example, as part of a tax planning strategy for infant children or an asset protection strategy for adult children.

In future posts we will look at other aspects of binding nominations, including non lapsing nominations.

Superannuation and binding death benefit nominations (BDBN)

Posted 14 February 2012

A couple of weeks ago there was a post in relation to superannuation nominations.

As mentioned in that post, where there is a valid BDBN, the trustee has no discretion to pay death benefits other than in accordance with the notice.

Based on recent client situations we have seen, a few critical points to remember in this area include the following –

(1) If a member's circumstances change and they have failed to update their BDBN, it will, subject in some situations to automatic lapsing (for example, every three years), continue to be binding on the trustee.
(2) The trust deed for the superannuation fund must allow for a BDBN to be given to the trustee of the fund – even some recently set up deeds do not always have such a provision.
(3) Unless specifically provided for in the deed, a BDBN will often need to be 'refreshed' every three years. An alternate approach is to update the trust deed for the fund to 'hardwire' the nomination into the deed, avoiding the requirement to regularly refresh the nomination.

Corporate trustees and SMSFs

5 November 2013

Many specialist advisers to self managed superannuation funds (SMSFs) recommend the use of a corporate trustee, as opposed to individual trustees.

While the initial setup costs of a corporate trustee are generally higher than individuals, there are a range of reasons that the use of a company is beneficial, including:

(1) as other posts have demonstrated, the use of a corporate trustee provides limited liability protection. This can be particularly important if the SMSF owns real property;
(2) special purpose corporate trustees of an SMSF are entitled to discounted annual ASIC fees;
(3) record keeping and compliance is significantly improved with a special purpose corporate trustee in terms of what the auditor (and ultimately the Tax Office) expects to see;
(4) from a succession planning perspective, it is significantly easier to regulate the control of a corporate trustee (i.e. by simply changing the directors from time to time) as opposed to individual trustees, where each time an individual trustee changes, there is often a myriad of documentation that needs preparing and notifications that must be made; and
(5) particularly in relation to sole member funds, the use of a corporate trustee significantly simplifies the overall structure of a SMSF, as a sole director company is permissible. In contrast, it is impossible to create a valid

SMSF with an individual trustee and sole member (there must always be an additional individual who acts as a co-trustee in this instance).

Estate Planning Costs Paid Through Superannuation

Posted 28 January 2014

It is well understood that, in order to obtain the concessional taxation available for superannuation savings, a superannuation fund must have its sole purpose as being the provision of benefits to members on retirement, or their dependants or legal personal representative (LPR) on death.

In this context, one issue that is often raised is whether a superannuation fund can pay the costs of ensuring its members have their estate planning affairs in order.

In the absence of any specific guidance from the Tax Office in this area, there are a range of views about the legitimacy of this approach.

Some advisers believe that any estate planning related expense is clearly incurred in order to help provide for the dependants or LPR of a member and therefore properly payable by a superannuation fund.

The conservative position is that either all estate planning costs should be incurred by members personally, or alternatively where they may be paid by the superannuation fund, there must be a direct and clear nexus between the expense incurred and the ultimate provision of benefits to dependants or LPR on the death of a member.

Next week's post will consider some specific examples of the types of costs that may be legitimately incurred by a superannuation fund on behalf of a member.

Costs Paid Via Superannuation

Posted 4 February 2014

Last week's post looked at the debate surrounding the incurring of estate planning costs by superannuation funds.

While the conservative approach seems to be that all estate planning costs should be incurred by members personally, practically, there are a number of examples where having a superannuation fund incur the relevant expense would appear reasonably arguable, including:

(1) where a superannuation trust deed is being updated as part of an estate planning exercise, clearly these costs should be incurred by the fund;
(2) where, as part of the update, binding nominations are prepared (either on a standalone basis or 'hardwired' into the trust deed), then again these costs are legitimately payable by the fund;
(3) where superannuation makes up a significant component of a member's overall wealth and the member intends (either via binding or non-binding nominations) for their superannuation entitlements to pass via their will, then the costs of the will (including any testamentary trusts incorporated into the documentation) should also be able to be paid by the fund;
(4) strategic advice to members in relation to the impact of death on their superannuation entitlements should also be properly payable by the fund; and
(5) while the nexus might be slightly less obvious, ensuring that a member has a legal personal representative able to take over the trusteeship of a self managed super fund may also justify a fund incurring costs for implementing a member's enduring power of attorney.

As with many similar topics, the general position outlined above will depend on the particular factual situation and the approach adopted by the advisers and firms directly assisting superannuation fund members in these areas.

Estate Planning 101 with Superannuation Entitlements

Posted 18 February 2014

Last week, I was again reminded of the very strange way in which the superannuation laws currently operate concerning death benefits, and more particularly, the distinction between someone withdrawing their superannuation on the day before death as opposed to it being paid out as a death benefit.

All other things being equal, it is often very likely to be the case that a withdrawal immediately before death will be completely free of tax, whereas the same funds distributed as a death benefit can be liable for tax of up to 30% (plus Medicare).

Obviously, there are a range of competing issues that need to be considered as part of any superannuation and estate planning exercise, however we are certainly seeing an increasing number of people more seriously consider the total amount they wish to retain in super in their later years.

Receipt of Superannuation Death Benefits

Posted 25 February 2014

Following a recent post, I had a number of enquiries, and one particular adviser raised an issue with me which (as she flagged) is often overlooked.

The particular issue relates to the payment of superannuation benefits on death. The legislation requires (and there have been cases supporting this) that the recipient of any death benefit must be alive on the date of the payment themselves – in other words, if the recipient is no longer living at the date the payment is ultimately due to be made, then neither they (nor their estate) will be entitled to receive it.

There are a number of ways to minimise the impact of this rule, however the steps must always be taken as part of the overall estate plan.

Death Benefit Nominations – Read the Deed

Posted 4 March 2014

Following on from recent posts concerning superannuation death benefit payments, I was reminded this week of the absolute importance of reading the superannuation trust deed before making any death benefit payment.

It is becoming more and more regular to see many people, as part of their overall estate plan, embedding their required superannuation distribution provisions into the superannuation trust deed. Where this is done, the fact that there might be other nominations, or even provisions in a person's will, not be of any effect – rather the terms of the deed must be followed.

In a future post, I will touch on a related issue concerning binding nominations that are entrenched in superannuation trust deeds.

Double Entrenching Binding Nominations

Posted 11 March 2014

In a recent post, we touched on the importance of reviewing a trust deed before making any superannuation death benefit payments.

The 'read the deed' mantra, which is so often used in the context of family trusts, is of similar importance in relation to self managed superannuation funds.

One particular provision to be aware of in this regard is that, even if a nomination (which appears to be binding) is embedded under the deed, unless the provision of that deed has a prohibition against amendment, the intentions of the parties may not in fact be achieved.

For example, the remaining trustees after death could elect to vary the deed (and effectively remove the binding nomination) before ultimately making a death benefit payment.

Super Deed Variations and Resettlements

Posted 18 March 2014

Last week we had an adviser, probably quite rightly, question us as to why a superannuation trust deed could be totally revoked and replaced with a completely new document, while changes to a family trust deed tend to be extremely piecemeal.

The issue can be largely answered by reference to the Tax Office's approach to resettlements.

Broadly, the Tax Office accepts that in relation to superannuation funds, a resettlement for tax purposes will never occur. Due to this approach (and stamp duty exemptions that apply in essentially every Australian state), most advisers recommend that when updating a superannuation trust deed, it is best to adopt a completely new deed.

In contrast, where updating a family trust deed, because of the risks associated from a resettlement perspective, it is usually best to only amend the provisions that are in particular need of being addressed.

Accelerated Superannuation Contributions

Posted 28 May 2014

Again this week we have had an article featured in the Weekly Tax Bulletin. This time it is by fellow View Legal Director Tara Lucke and I and is extracted below for those who do not otherwise have easy access.

If is often said, there is nothing certain in life but death and taxes… and adjustments to the limits for superannuation contributions. In recent times, particularly given the ongoing adjustments to the limits for concessional superannuation contributions, the way in which to maximise contributions has been an area of focus.

Overview

As is well understood, concessional contributions to superannuation can generally be made by:

a an employer of a member;
b a member; and
c the spouse of the member.

The rules in relation to the quantum of permissible concessional contributions (historically referred to as deductible contributions) have been subject to regular change. The changes have primarily focused on the dollar limit for contributions made in each financial year.

Concessional contributions which currently count towards the annual concessional limit include:

a all employer contributions (eg super guarantee, salary sacrifice);
b member contributions which are claimed as a tax deduction; and
c in some situations, allocations from any fund reserves.

Concessional contribution limits

The maximum amount of concessional contributions that may be paid for the 2014-15 year of income without being subject to excess contributions tax were confirmed at 2014 WTB 9 [286] as follows:

a $30,000 per annum per person aged under 49 years on 30 June 2014;
b $35,000 per annum per person aged 49 years and over on 30 June 2014.

These limits have been increased, by way of "stepped" indexation, for the first time since the current contribution limit regime was introduced and are unlikely to be indexed again for at least 3 years.

Non-concessional contribution limits

Subject to potential variations by adopting one of the accelerated contribution approaches explained below, the maximum non concessional limits for the 2014-15 year of income (without being subject to excess contributions tax), have also been increased for indexation and are now as follows:

a $180,000 per annum per person (for contributions on or after 1 July 2014); and
b $540,000 per person averaged over three years (if a 3 year contribution was started before 1 July 2014, then the limit remains $450,000).

Accelerated contributions

Historically, when the per annum limit was capped at $150,000 (and the 3-year average at $450,000), the main strategies available in relation accelerating contributions have been best exemplified by the following table:

Member age	61	62	63	64	65	Total
Financial year	2013/14	2014/15	2015/16	2016/17	2017/18	Contributions
Scenario 1	$150,000	$150,000	$150,000	$150,000	$150,000*	$750,000
Scenario 2	$150,000	$150,000	$450,000	Nil	Nil	$750,000
Scenario 3	$150,000	$150,000	$150,000	$450,000	Nil	$900,000
Scenario 4	$450,000	Nil	Nil	$450,000	Nil	$900,000
Scenario 5	$150,000	$450,000	Nil	Nil	$450,000#	$1,050,000
Scenario 6	$150,000	$150,000	$150,000	$150,000	$450,000*	$1,050,000

In relation to the above table (and the further table below), it is important to note the following:

1 *Assuming contributions are made prior to member's 65th birthday or made after reaching age 65 and the member continues to satisfy the required gainful employment test.
2 #Assuming contributions are made prior to member's 65th birthday or the member was aged 65 at any time in the year and continues to satisfy the required gainful employment test or the contributions were made after the member's 65th birthday.

With the changed superannuation thresholds commencing on 1 July 2014 (again as noted at 2014 WTB 9 [286]), it will be important to reference an updated version of the table, as set out below.

Critically, the updated table assumes that the first contribution is made after 1 July 2014.

As set out in the earlier article, if a combined contribution is commenced before 1 July 2014, the previous table continues to apply until the accelerated approach is completed.

Member age	**61**	**62**	**63**	**64**	**65**	**Total**
Financial year	**2014/15**	**2015/16**	**2016/17**	**2017/18**	**2018/19**	**Contributions**
Scenario 1	$180,000	$180,000	$180,000	$180,000	$180,000*	$900,000
Scenario 2	$180,000	$180,000	$540,000	Nil	Nil	$900,000
Scenario 3	$180,000	$180,000	$180,000	$540,000	Nil	$1,080,000
Scenario 4	$540,000	Nil	Nil	$540,000	Nil	$1,080,000
Scenario 5	$180,000	$540,000	Nil	Nil	$540,000#	$1,260,000
Scenario 6	$180,000	$180,000	$180,000	$180,000	$540,000*	$1,260,000

1 *Assuming contributions are made prior to member's 65th birthday or made after reaching age 65 and the member continues to satisfy the required gainful employment test.

2 #Assuming contributions are made prior to member's 65th birthday or the member was aged 65 at any time in the year and continues to satisfy the required gainful employment test or the contributions were made after the member's 65th birthday.

As a comparison of the 2 tables clearly illustrates, in many client situations there will be a significant differential in delaying non concessional contributions until 1 July 2014 to take advantage of the increased thresholds.

Accessing disablement proceeds via superannuation

Posted 26 August 2014

This week's post addresses an issue recently raised with us by an adviser, focussing on the ability to access insurance proceeds from a superannuation fund on an event of permanent incapacity.

The particular issue raised involved the fact that best practice often dictates that clients should obtain insurance protection on the basis of an inability to work in their 'own', as opposed to 'any' occupation.

The satisfaction of the 'own' occupation test is obviously easier than the condition of release set out under the superannuation legislation, being that a member must be incapable of working in 'any' occupation.

Where insurance is owned via a superannuation fund there is therefore a risk that while the fund will receive an insurance payout, it will be unable to release it to the member until some other condition of release is satisfied (for example, reaching the retirement age).

Historically therefore, the conservative view was undoubtedly that own occupation insurance should always be owned outside super. Importantly, since 1 July 2014, own occupation insurance is no longer available via superannuation, subject to a grandfathering for arrangements already in place before that date.

For those pre-existing arrangements, there appears to be a pragmatic approach adopted, particularly by those with policies via a self-managed superannuation fund. This approach involves assuming that a trustee (who will also be a member of the relevant fund) will adopt a liberal interpretation of the 'any' occupation definition under the superannuation legislation and therefore always allow the release of insurance proceeds.

Division 152 concessions and superannuation contributions

Posted 17 February 2015

Given the number of changes to the small business concessions since their introduction back in 1997, it is understandable that many clients and their advisers lose track of the exact way in which the provisions work.

Last week, we were reminded when assisting another adviser about one critical aspect of the rules, namely that in many instances it is possible for taxpayers to delay a decision on whether to roll a capital gain over into a new asset, pay the tax, or make a contribution into superannuation for at least two years after the date of sale. Indeed in many cases the deferral opportunity is closer to three years.

Obviously (as with most aspects of the small business concessions), care needs to be taken to ensure this planning opportunity is in fact available, however assuming the basic conditions are otherwise satisfied, the additional two to three year window is one that we are seeing regularly accessed.

Division 152 and the turnover test

Posted 7 April 2015

Following on from a recent post about the small business capital gains tax concessions, one adviser made contact in relation to an additional planning opportunity that is often overlooked.

In particular, where a business satisfies the $2 million turnover test, it can be possible that the $6 million net asset test is ignored.

Where the $2 million turnover test is satisfied, there is no need to apply the $6 million net asset test. In other words, the total value of the assets involved is effectively ignored.

Particularly in relation to agribusiness clients, the turnover test can provide a significant benefit that would otherwise be unavailable if the net asset test needed to also be satisfied.

Why superannuation proceeds trusts should only be an avenue of last resort

Posted 2 June 2015

A 2014 post touched on the use of a superannuation proceeds trust (**SPT**) – ***http://blog.viewlegal.com.au/2014/09/what-are-superannuation-proceeds-trusts.html***

The question arose because of a decision to avoid establishing testamentary trusts on the death of one spouse.

As identified recently by one adviser we work with, such an approach was arguably not appropriate in all the circumstances because:

(1) SPTs are generally a structure of last resort. This is for a combination of reasons, not least of which because under superannuation law there is no clear pathway to allow a superannuation trustee to distribute to a SPT; and
(2) Conversely under taxation law, unless the money passes directly from the superannuation fund into the SPT, there is a real risk that the Tax Office will not allow access to the excepted trust income provisions.

For these reasons it is generally preferable that the funds are paid to the legal personal representative and then distributed under the will into a testamentary discretionary trust which is crafted in a way to create a 'sub-trust' in relation to the superannuation proceeds.

This approach ensures that the surviving spouse will have the flexibility to have all funds in a trust environment while also ensuring the proceeds are received tax free into the estate.

Superannuation proceeds trusts

Posted 9 June 2015

Following last week's post an issue has been raised as to whether our wills provide for a Superannuation Proceeds Trust (**SPT**) –and the answer is: yes they do.

A SPT within a will (as opposed to last week's post that related to a structure established outside a will) is a trust that is set up solely to receive the superannuation benefits of a member following death.

Generally, the beneficiaries of a SPT must be confined to persons who are 'death benefit dependants' of the deceased, being a:

a spouse or former spouse of the deceased;
b child, aged below 18, of the deceased;
c person with whom the deceased had an 'interdependency relationship'; or
d person financially dependent on the deceased just before they died.

The benefits of having a SPT in a will are:

(1) it provides greater asset protection compared to the superannuation death benefits being paid directly to a death benefit dependant – for example, against relationship breakdowns, creditors or spendthrift beneficiaries;

(2) distributions from the SPT will generally be excepted trust income, such that recipients under the age of 18 will be treated as adults;
(3) the distribution of the superannuation death benefits to the SPT is taxed in the same way as if they had been paid directly to the death benefit dependant (provided the beneficiaries of the SPT are limited to tax dependants).

Next week we will look in more detail at how View Legal structures SPTs in wills.

View Legal and superannuation proceeds trusts

Posted 16 June 2015

Last week's post explained the broad requirements and main benefits of a Superannuation Proceeds Trust (**SPT**) established under a will. This week's post focuses on how View Legal's testamentary trust (**TT**) wills deal with any superannuation benefits that are paid to a will maker's estate.

Generally, the range of potential beneficiaries listed under a TT are wider than dependants for tax purposes. The way in which View Legal crafts its TTs however gives the trustee complete discretion about which of the beneficiaries may receive any superannuation benefits available for distribution.

In particular, the terms of the will allow the trustee to essentially establish a 'sub trust' of the TT for receipt of the superannuation proceeds – with the only beneficiaries being those who satisfy the definition of a tax dependant.

In this way, the various benefits of having a SPT, as outlined in last week's post, can be achieved.

Incapacity and SMSF control

Posted 7 July 2015

Where a member of an SMSF dies, leaving (for example) their spouse as the sole member and a reversionary pensioner, issues can arise where that member themselves loses capacity.

In this scenario, much depends on the exact circumstances including the timing of the various death/incapacity events and whether the SMSF has an individual or corporate trustee. Broadly, where corporate trustee is in place:

(1) Upon the death of the first member (leaving a reversionary pension for the other member), the remaining member would control the SMSF as sole director of the corporate trustee. The executor for the deceased member would not have any ongoing involvement in the SMSF or corporate trustee.
(2) Upon the subsequent incapacity of the second member, their financial power of attorney would, subject to the exact provisions of both the SMSF deed and the constitution for the corporate trustee, have the ability to remove the incapacitated director and appoint themselves in their place.
(3) While there must be an enduring power of attorney in place before the event of incapacity, there is no specific wording required in the document itself, rather the SMSF deed and the constitution will be critical.
(4) The attorney for the incapacitated member would then perform the administrative functions in their capacity as director of the corporate trustee.

Superannuation proceeds trusts: Tricks and traps

Posted 21 July 2015

For those that do not otherwise have access to theWeekly Tax Bulletin, the further article from earlier this month by fellowView LegalDirector Patrick Ellwood and me is extracted below. It provides a more technical analysis of the various issues surrounding superannuation proceeds trusts, building on the discussion in recent posts.

A superannuation proceeds trust (**SPT**) is a trust established solely to receive superannuation proceeds on the death of a fund member. A SPT can be established by a will or by deed after the death of an individual, although establishing the structure post death can be problematic and is outside the scope of this article.

The ITAA 1997 provides that a superannuation death benefit, paid to a death benefit dependant as a lump sum, is not assessable income. A death benefit dependant (defined under s 302-195 of the ITAA 1997) is a:

- spouse or former spouse of the deceased;
- child, aged below 18, of the deceased;
- person with whom the deceased had an "interdependency relationship", as defined by s 302-200 of the ITAA 1997; or
- person financially dependent on the deceased just before they died.

Payments to the estate

Where there are death benefit dependants under a deceased estate who are potential recipients of superannuation benefits, it is often an appropriate estate planning strategy to allow for a separate SPT under the will in addition to any testamentary trust (**TT**), so that a tax-free distribution of the superannuation proceeds can be achieved via a protected structure. Other estate assets can be distributed to a TT that has beneficiaries who are not death benefit dependants.

When the superannuation proceeds are paid to a SPT, the legal personal representative (**LPR**) is taxed in accordance with how the person or persons intended to benefit from the estate would be taxed were they to have received the payments directly. That is, ATO will generally adopt a "look through" approach as if the death benefit had been paid directly to the recipient.

To ensure that any receipt of superannuation proceeds is tax-free, the LPR should ensure that, at least at the time of receipt of the superannuation proceeds by the SPT, the only capital beneficiaries of the SPT are those who meet the definition of "death benefit dependant" under s 302-195 of the ITAA 1997.

In practical terms, this means that where there is more than one death benefit dependant, the terms of the SPT should provide that they receive the trust capital in specified shares on vesting.

In particular, ATO Interpretative Decision 2001/751 (which has since been withdrawn on the basis that its view has been subsumed into s 302-10 of the ITAA 1997) confirms that it appears to be the clear intention of the legislation that the fact that a payment is made to a trustee, rather than directly to the dependant, should not obscure the fact that the payment is ultimately for the benefit of the dependant.

In the facts considered in ATO ID 2001/751, the death benefit dependant was the sole beneficiary of the trust and, therefore, absolutely entitled to the income and capital of the trust.

Income beneficiaries of a SPT

The requirement that death benefit dependants receive the capital on the ending of the trust is also driven by the requirements of s 102AG(2) of the ITAA 1936, which sets out the basis on which trust property must be regulated when the trust ends, in order to access the excepted trust income provisions. The excepted trust income provisions effectively allow infant beneficiaries of income distributions to be taxed as adults.

There is limited guidance about whether the ATO will require all the income beneficiaries of a SPT to be death benefit dependants.

The conservative position would be to limit the income beneficiaries of the SPT to death benefit dependants only. In particular, the guidance available in relation to whether tax will be payable on receipt of the superannuation proceeds under s 302-10 of the ITAA 1997 indicates that the income and capital beneficiaries should be limited to death benefit dependants.

It is arguable however, based on the ATO's comments in Taxation Ruling TR 98/4, that a SPT can include a broad range of discretionary income beneficiaries. While TR 98/4 sets out the ATO's view in relation to child maintenance trusts (see 2015 WTB 11 [287]), it can by analogy be argued that the comments apply to other similar types of trusts (including SPTs).

Furthermore, in practical terms, it appears that the ATO only tests the range of potential beneficiaries of the SPT at the date at which the superannuation proceeds are received by the SPT (for example, see private ruling authorisation number 1011741138466).

Therefore, even if a trustee takes the conservative approach, that is, to limit the range of potential income beneficiaries to death benefit dependants, following receipt of the proceeds, it may be possible for the range of beneficiaries to be expanded to include non-death benefit dependants.

Provisions of a will

For completeness, as superannuation proceeds do not automatically form part of the estate of the deceased member, it may be necessary to ensure that appropriate nominations are made by the member to direct that the superannuation death benefits are paid to the LPR for distribution under the will, and if appropriate, to any SPT established.

Assuming proceeds are paid under a will, the LPR should have the power to ensure that the range of potential beneficiaries can be limited to persons:

- within the provisions of s 295-485(1)(a) of the ITAA 1997; and
- who satisfy the definition of "death benefits dependant" under s 302-195 of the ITAA 1997.

The main reason both these provisions should be mentioned is due to the requirement under s 295-485(4) that regard needs to be had to the extent to which a death benefit dependant can reasonably be expected to benefit from the estate.

In particular, s 295-485 of the ITAA 1997 gives superannuation funds the ability to claim a tax deduction based on an increased amount of superannuation lump sum death benefit paid under the "anti-detriment" rules, with reference to the tax paid on contributions.

Conclusion

In many respects, the ability to utilise a SPT under a will incorporating a TT is a simple, yet powerful, strategy that practically is useful in a large range of circumstances.

There are however some fundamental threshold issues that need to be addressed to ensure the expected income tax concessions can be validly accessed. Furthermore, given the significant number of estate planning related issues aside from tax that are potentially relevant, it is critical that a methodical approach is adopted.

Chapter 9

ADVISER TOOLS

ATO feedback on taxpayer alerts

Posted 30 September 2010

Many of you will have seen the recently released minutes from the National Tax Liaison Group meeting held on 23 June.

One item of interest relates to the ATO's view on taxpayer alerts (TA).

In particular, the ATO claims that TAs are simply intended as an 'early warning' to taxpayers and their advisers of significant new and emerging higher risk tax planning issues or arrangements the ATO has under risk assessment.

The ATO claims TAs are essentially a 'press release' about issues causing it concern which it releases 'in the interests of an open tax administration'. The ATO stressed that TAs are not expected to replace rulings, and are not meant to be an ATO view of the law.

The ATO acknowledged the concern about the perceived scope of some of its issued TAs. To address this issue, the ATO undertook to focus on 'ensuring the mischief is more clearly identified to allay any concerns that tax professionals and the wider community may have about the generality of the application' of TAs.

What exactly is a firm of the future?

Posted 6 February 2012

Many regular readers will be aware that for around ten years now we have charged on the basis of scoping work up front and providing a set price – that is no time billing.

A large part of the inspiration for abandoning time billing came from the landmark publication 'Firm of the Future' by Ron Baker and Paul Dunn. That book describes a journey from the traditional (and largely archaic) professional service firm model to being a knowledge firm. Understanding the value that knowledge workers create and having the skills to price without any reference to time is the foundation of the journey.

While subsequent publications by Baker (in particular 'Pricing on Purpose' and the more recent 'Implementing Value Pricing') provide significant guidance, we have found that the ability to listen and interact with likeminded advisers who are wanting to consider (or have started) the journey to a life without timesheets is invaluable.

To learn more, more about the opportunities available in this regard please contact me.

Verasage 'TED'

Posted 20 February 2012

As part of the thought leadership event facilitated by the Verasage Group in early 2011, I had the opportunity to present a 'TED' style presentation on the evolution of the Australia's first virtual law firm platform which was the precursor to the foundation in 2014 of View Legal.

A link to the presentation – ***https://www.youtube.com/watch?v=JNnnbkfXY84***

War stories

Posted 23 July 2012

As many regular readers will be aware, examples are often used in these posts and our various seminar presentations based on client situations.

This said, unless the particular client scenario has gone through the court system (and is therefore publicly available information), we are always very careful to not base our examples entirely on any one particular client so as to ensure client confidentiality is maintained.

In this context then, we are also always supportive of any adviser that wants to use (and where appropriate embellish) case study examples that we may have historically shared when they are positioning concepts with clients.

Alternative RSS readers to Google Reader

Posted 13 August 2013

With Google Reader shutting down last month, I thought it was a good time to remind followers about alternative RSS readers. The most popular Google Reader alternative is Feedly (iOS/Android/Web) as it is an easy way to follow all of your blog and other RSS feeds in one place.

Here is a good article for alternative RSS readers that you might find helpful:

http://lifehacker.com/google-reader-is-shutting-down-here-are-the-best-alter-5990456

If you are not familiar with RSS Readers, you may prefer to subscribe to the blog via email. To subscribe to the blog, please enter your email address in the subscription box in the right hand column.

You can also follow me through social media on Twitter and other platforms which are all linked on my About Me page for your convenience.

Redline changes

24 September 2013

At the moment, we are assisting a client in relation to the sale of shares in their trading company.

Last week, we received suggested changes to the share sale agreement for the lawyers acting for the purchaser.

As is usual commercial practice, this top tier law firm provided the document to us confirming that all of their suggested changes were made in 'redline'. While we had no particular reason to doubt that all changes would have been shown in mark-up, we used the 'delta view' function in Word to be certain of this before commencing our review.

The delta view confirmed that while almost all changes were shown in redline, there were a handful of words changed to one particular clause in the warranties that had not been marked up. These words (if gone undetected) would have potentially left our client in an unnecessarily weak position following settlement.

As we understand it, the oversight of not marking up these changes was a simple mistake, however it highlights the importance of always using the delta view function regardless of whether the amendments are otherwise promised to have been marked up.

Two View Legal iPhone and Android apps launched

Posted 5 August 2014

Based on feedback from advisers, View Legal has recently developed and launched two new iPhone and Android apps.

Each app can be downloaded via the following links –

(1) iPhone Directors' Duties – ***https://itunes.apple.com/us/app/directors-duties/id902289581?ls=1&mt=8***

(2) Android Directors' Duties – *https://play.google.com/store/apps/details?id=director.duties*
(3) iPhone Estate planning – *https://itunes.apple.com/us/app/view-legal-estate-planning/id902301642?ls=1&mt=8*
(4) Android Estate planning – *https://play.google.com/store/apps/details?id=view.legal.estate.planning*

Directors' Duties App

Acting as a director of a company imposes many obligations and duties.

The directors' duties app is designed to allow the user to help narrow down some of the broad areas that might be relevant in relation to their current or any intended directorships.

Depending on the answers provided, the app generates a free white paper that sets out general information about numerous aspects of the duties directors have.

Estate Planning App

Estate planning is the process of ensuring wealth is dealt with, after death, as intended, while minimising the impact of challenges against the arrangements and costs such as stamp duty, tax and administration expenses.

The estate planning app is designed to allow the user to help narrow down some of the broad areas that might be relevant in relation to implementing, or updating, an estate plan.

Again, depending on the answers provided, the app generates a free white paper that sets out general information about a range of estate planning strategies.

Latest View Legal Apple and Android app launched

Posted 4 November 2014

Following the successful launch earlier this year of the View Legal Directors Duties and Estate Planning apps, we have now developed and launched another Apple and Android app.

The new app is in relation to Business Succession and can be downloaded via the following links –

(1) iPhone –
https://itunes.apple.com/au/app/business-succession/id927283653?mt=8
(2) Android–
https://play.google.com/store/apps/details?id=business.succession

Business succession is the important process of ensuring a plan is in place for a person's business assets so they are dealt with, after death, as intended, while minimising the impact of challenges against the arrangements and costs such as stamp duty, tax and administration expenses.

The business succession area is however heavily regulated and it is vital that business owners and their advisers have a deep understanding across all relevant areas.

The business succession app is designed to allow the user to narrow down some of the broad areas that might be relevant in relation to a business succession plan.

Depending on the answers provided, the app generates a free white paper containing general information in relation to some of the issues that are often relevant.

Another View Legal Apple and Android app launched

Posted 18 November 2014

Following the successful launch earlier this year of the View Legal Directors Duties, Estate Planning and business succession apps, we have now developed and launched a further Apple and Android app.

The new app is in relation to binding death benefit nominations (**BDBN**) and can be downloaded via the following links –

(1) iPhone – *https://itunes.apple.com/au/app/bdbn/id931237201?mt=8*
(2) Android –
https://play.google.com/store/apps/details?id=view.legal.bdbn

BDBNs can be an essential tool for anyone with superannuation savings. BDBNs are however heavily regulated and there are many aspects that can cause irreversible damage if misunderstood.

The app explores some of the fundamental issues that arise for anyone with superannuation savings considering making a BDBN.

Depending on the answers provided, the app generates a free white paper containing general information in relation to some of the issues that are often relevant.

And another View Legal Apple and Android app launched

Posted 2 December 2014

Following the successful launch earlier this year of the View Legal Directors Duties, Estate Planning, business succession and binding death benefit nomination apps, we have now developed and launched a further Apple and Android app.

The new app is in relation to Self-managed superannuation funds (**SMSF**) and can be downloaded via the following links –

(1) iPhone – ***https://itunes.apple.com/au/app/smsf/id931264885?mt=8***
(2) Android– ***https://play.google.com/store/apps/details?id=view.legal.smsf***

SMSFs can provide a range of benefits and opportunities not available via any other retirement savings approach.

SMSFs are however heavily regulated and it is vital that fund members have a deep understanding across all relevant areas.

The SMSF app is designed to allow the user to narrow down some of the broad areas that might be relevant in relation to establishing, or updating, an SMSF.

Depending on the answers provided, the app generates a free white paper containing general information in relation to some of the issues that are often relevant.

The Privacy Act and View Legal's international footprint

Posted 3 February 2015

A key component of the View Legal platform has been its dedication to early adoption of innovations that can help achieve the reason we built the platform – to create the kind of firm our friends would choose to use.

The 2014 changes to the privacy rules requiring more detailed disclosure of businesses' international footprint is a timely opportunity for us to revisit the extent of the contribution made to the View Legal platform from around the world.

Like most businesses, our success essentially depends on a network of specialists. As a law firm, we have an agreement with each service provider that receives personal client information which requires that they comply with the Australian privacy legislation.

A summary of our virtual team currently (although it sometimes changes on a weekly basis) is as follows:

(1) we have lawyers based in the Philippines, regional Queensland, India, South Africa and suburban Brisbane.
(2) our IT team has contributors in the Brisbane CBD, various locations throughout India and suburban Brisbane, together with cloud supported services throughout the USA and other confidential locations.
(3) our marketing and collateral providers are sourced from various locations throughout Europe, USA, Canada, New Zealand, the Philippines and Australia.
(4) one of our favourite social media consultants currently assists from suburban Brisbane, other than when she is travelling in locations such as Buenos Aires, Spain, Italy, Greece, the UK, France and Germany.
(5) one of our research consultants currently works out of Argentina.
(6) we have copy editors based in New South Wales, Victoria, the US and the UK.
(7) we have administrative and accounting support from assistants in the Philippines, New Zealand, Canada, Pakistan and Sweden.
(8) our primary word processing provider, who has been a critical part of our success, even in the years prior to View Legal launching, is based in India.

As the popularity of platforms such as Elance and Fiverr (that we have used extensively from their launch) continues to grow, we suspect the only certainty for our business is that our international footprint will also continue to grow.

This said, the growth of our international team has been matched by the growth of our Australian based team, and we take great pride in the fact that all staff enjoy flexibility around their work arrangements, and work remotely with access to physical office space on a needs basis only.

The Art of Value

Posted 5 May 2015

Many would be aware of our passion for up front, guaranteed fixed pricing rather than the traditional time-billing model of most law firms.

A summary of our approach in this regard has received wide spread interest – see the 'Old View v New View' table on our website at –

http://viewlegal.com.au/a-new-view/

Much of our inspiration in this regard comes from the VeraSage Institute, a revolutionary international think tank which, for many years, has been challenging professional services firms to price their services other than with reference to the Marxist derived labour theory of value that is time billing.

The VeraSage Institute was founded by LinkedIn Influencer Ron Baker and we are proud to be listed as a VeraSage 'Trailblazer' (see – ***http://www.verasage.com/thelist/***).

Another of the Trailblazers listed is the business from the United States founded by Kirk Bowman known as 'The Art of Value'.

Kirk hosts a podcast on iTunes and recently I was fortunate enough to be featured on it.

A link to the podcast is as follows – ***https://itunes.apple.com/au/podcast/art-value-show-discover-value/id924824616?mt=2#episodeGuid=http%3A%2F%2Fartofvalue.com%2F%3Fp%3D4849***. Alternatively it can be viewed via the Art of Value blog, that also provides session notes at – ***http://artofvalue.com/journey-from-time-to-value-matthew-burgess/***

The interview touches on many aspects of our experience, including:

(1) That value pricing is a journey, not a destination;
(2) Case study examples of fixed pricing by professional services;
(3) The importance of agreeing with a client a defined scope before commencing work;
(4) That while fixed pricing may change your business, offering customers choices can change your life;
(5) Exploring the cultural issues behind converting from a time billing firm (where the key focus is on what is 'chargeable') to a timeless firm (where the key focus is on what is valuable).

Latest View Legal Apple and Android app launched

Posted 26 May 2015

Following the successful launch last year of 5 View legal apps (in areas such as estate planning, business succession and SMSFs), we have now developed and launched another Apple and Android app.

The new app is in relation tocreating a template Memorandum of Directions (MoD) and canbe downloaded via the following links –

(1) Apple– ***https://appsto.re/au/7ayT6.i***

(2) Android– ***https://play.google.com/store/apps/details?id=view.legal.mod***

A MoD can be an essential estate planning tool.

Importantly however, MoDs are generally only morally (not legally) binding and therefore do not change the provisions of a will.

The View Legal MoD app is designed to allow the user to narrow down some of the broad areas that might be relevant in relation to implementing, or updating, their MoD.

Depending on the answers provided, the app generates a free template memorandum of directions in PDF and word, allowing the user to then use this as a framework to complete the document as they wish.

Apple iTunes Podcasts launched by View

Posted 4 August 2015

Leveraging our successful webinar series, View is excited to announce the launch of our iTunes podcast channel.

In creating this new service we have joined the thousands of public and commercial broadcasters, renowned celebrities and independent podcasters on iTunes giving you immediate free access via your iphone, ipad or computer to specialist content across a range of topics.

Each podcast contains 60 minutes of audio content from View's various webinar and seminar programs. The podcasts can be found on our website at the following link – ***http://viewlegal.com.au/view-legal-podcast/*** or directly on iTunes – simply search 'View Legal'.

Podcasts already released include –

a Failed Trust Distributions
b Estate planning and asset protection
c Superannuation and estate planning
d Are you ready for June 30?
e Testamentary trusts – the fundamentals

Making our webinars available as podcasts offers yet another mode of accessing specialist content and the ability to 'try before you buy' –recordings giving access to the full video presentation of each webinar and seminar are also available via our website in DVD, USB and streaming formats – see

http://viewlegal.com.au/recorded-webinars/

New View podcasts will be released on iTunes every few weeks, so consider subscribing for automatic notification.

2015 Legal Innovation Index

Posted 1 September 2015

As has been publicised elsewhere, Matthew Burgess on behalf of View, has won a place on the prestigious **2015 Legal Innovation Index** announced by LexisNexis and Janders Dean.

The award was in recognition of the View Intellectual Property (or VIP) platform – see –

http://viewlegal.com.au/view-vip-subscription-platform-2/

The VIP platform creates a compelling value proposition for virtually every professional service adviser who does any work in the estate planning, tax planning, asset protection, structuring and superannuation areas.

Importantly, it particularly creates access for advisers below partner, director and principal levels inside firms that traditionally have had no direct access to high quality legal solutions.

In turn, there is a 'ripple effect' for each of the advisers that subscribe that flows to their respective client base due to the increased access to quality and legal content from recognised specialists.

The platform also pays homage to its original inspiration such that every subscription sees View make charitable donations to the B1G1 platform (see – ***https://www.b1g1.com/buy1give1/***) and projects such as education support, clean water and medical attention in communities around the world.

B1G1 (Business for Good) is chaired by 4 times TEDx speaker Paul Dunn who has also been a passionate supporter of the VIP platform since learning of the original inspiration for it and the platform's ongoing commitment to giving back.

ABOUT THE AUTHOR

Matthew Burgess

Matthew Burgess co-founded specialist firm View Legal in 2014, having been a lawyer and partner of one of Australia's leading independent law firms for over 17 years.

Matthew's passion is helping clients successfully achieve their goals.

Matthew specialises in trusts, tax, estate and succession planning, providing strategic advice to business owners and high net worth individuals, and has been recognised in the 'Best Lawyers' list since 2014 in relation to trusts and estates and in 'Doyles' since 2015 for taxation.

While a significant focus of Matthew's practice is on small to medium enterprises and private business owners, the growth in this area in recent years has meant that he also regularly works on transactions with listed companies.

In part leveraging off the skills he has developed working in the SME market space, Matthew has been the catalyst in developing a number of innovative legal products for advisers and their clients; including establishing Australia's first virtual law firm.

Matthew presenters for many industry associations, accounting firms, financial advisers and commercial businesses, often speaking to the 'www' theme (why the wealthy win) . The www series of presentations builds on the lessons Matthew has taken while acting for a significant percentage of the members of BRW Rich List for the last decade.

In early 2006 he gave away the family television (effectively replicating for his children the TV free upbringing he had) . In his new found spare time, Matthew started publishing a collection of illustrated children's stories. These books are in addition to his published law related books, including 'Inside Stories' –the consolidated book of legal blog posts since 2010.

Acknowledgement

This book is the result of contributions from a number of people, each of whom I thank.

In particular:

(1) The team I work with at View Legal, provide an environment dedicated to continual improvement. Our sharing of knowledge as a team is reflected by the sharing of knowledge each week in the posts, that ultimately result in this publication.

(2) All members inspire me to do better each day, and particularly thank you goes to Naomi Arnold, Patrick Ellwood and Tara Lucke for constantly raising our standards from a legal perspective.

(3) Winnie Van has added significant value to the View Legal platform since foundation and before that for many years in various key roles.

(4) Finally, thank you to my family, for being on this journey with me.

www.ingramcontent.com/pod-product-compliance
Lightning Source LLC
LaVergne TN
LVHW022157200926
848481LV00006B/1776
* 9 7 8 1 9 2 5 4 0 6 0 8 5 *